Introduction to Our New NEAB

The Science Coordination Group was set up with the aim of producing specialised revision material for National Curriculum Science. Following popular demand we have taken our very successful Revision Guides for GCSE double science and from them produced a number of syllabus-specific versions for the NEAB and SEG double science syllabuses.

All of our Revision Guides exhibit several crucial features which set them apart from the rest:

1) Careful and Complete Explanations

Unlike other revision guides, we do not restrict ourselves to a brief outline of the bare essentials. Instead we work hard to give complete, concise and carefully written details on each topic.

2) Deliberate Use of Humour and Colourful Language

We consider the humour to be an essential part of our Revision Guides. It is there to keep the reader interested and entertained, and we are certain that it greatly assists their learning.
(It is not however expected to win us any awards...)

3) Carefully Matched to the NEAB Coordinated Syllabus, and more...

We have taken great care to ensure that this book follows the exact detail of the NEAB double award coordinated syllabus.
Once again however we feel that merely illustrating the syllabus is an inadequate approach.
We have therefore done rather more than simply list the basic syllabus details and add pictures.
Instead we have endeavoured to include all the relevant explanation which appears to us to be necessary. The result is a full 96 pages giving a clear explanation of the whole syllabus content.
We hope you will appreciate the amount of time and care which has gone into this.

Higher | This book is suitable for both Higher and Foundation Tier candidates.
The material which is required only for higher tier is clearly indicated in blue boxes like this.
In addition, the Higher Tier questions in the Revision Summaries are printed in blue. | Higher

And Keep Learning the Basic Facts...

Throughout these books there is constant emphasis on the inescapable need to keep *learning the basic facts*. This simple message is hammered home without compromise and without remorse, and whilst this traditionally brutal philosophy may not be quite in line with some other approaches to education, we still rather like it. But only because it works.

Contents

(NEAB Syllabus Section)

Published by Coordination Group Publications
Typesetting and Layout by The Science Coordination Group
Illustrations by: Sandy Gardner, e-mail: zimkit@aol.com

Consultant Editor: Paddy Gannon BSc MA

Printed by Hindson Print, Newcastle upon Tyne.

Solids, Liquids and Gases

These are known as the *three states of matter*. Make sure you know everything there is to know.

Solids have Strong Forces of Attraction

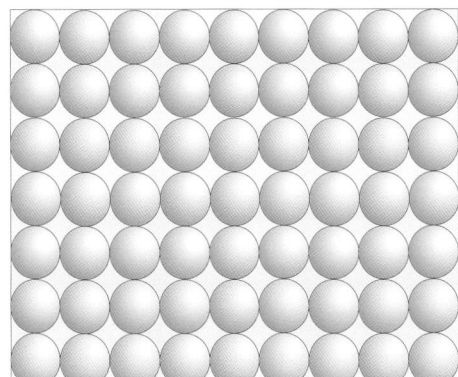

1) There are *strong forces* of *attraction* between molecules.
2) The molecules are held in *fixed positions* in a very regular lattice arrangement.
3) They *don't* move from their positions, so all solids keep a definite *shape* and *volume*, and don't flow like liquids.
4) They *vibrate* about their positions.
The *hotter* the solid becomes, the *more* they *vibrate*. This causes solids to *expand* slightly when heated.
5) Solids *can't be compressed* because the molecules are already packed *very* closely together.
6) Solids are generally *very* dense.

Liquids have Moderate Forces of Attraction

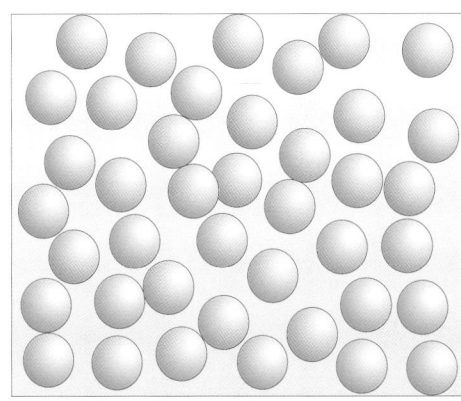

1) There is *some* force of *attraction* between the molecules.
2) The molecules are *free* to move past each other, but they do tend to *stick* together.
3) Liquids *don't* keep a *definite shape* and will flow to fill the bottom of a container. But they do keep the *same* volume.
4) The molecules are *constantly* moving in *random* motion.
The *hotter* the liquid becomes, the *faster* they move. This causes liquids to *expand* slightly when heated.
5) Liquids *can't* be compressed because the molecules are already packed *closely* together.
6) Liquids are *quite dense*, but not as dense as solids.

Gases have No Forces of Attraction

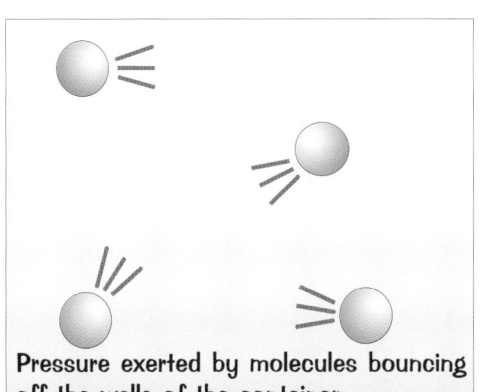

Pressure exerted by molecules bouncing off the walls of the container.

1) There is *no* force of *attraction* between the molecules.
2) The molecules are free to move. They travel in *straight lines* and only interact with each other when they *collide*.
3) Gases *don't* keep a *definite* shape or volume and will always *expand* to fill any container. Gases exert a *pressure* on the walls of the container.
4) The molecules are *constantly* moving in *random* motion.
The *hotter* the gas becomes, the *faster* they move. When *heated*, a gas will either *expand* or its *pressure* will *increase*.
5) *Gases* can be *compressed* easily because there's a lot of *free space* between the molecules.
6) Gases all have very low *densities*.

Don't get yourself in a state about this lot, just learn it...

This is pretty basic stuff, but people still lose marks in the Exam because they don't make sure to learn all the little details really thoroughly. And there's only one way to do that: *COVER THE PAGE UP AND SCRIBBLE IT ALL DOWN FROM MEMORY*. That soon shows what you really know — and that's what you've got to do for every page. Do it now for this one, *AND KEEP TRYING UNTIL YOU CAN*.

Changes of State

CHANGES OF STATE always involve *HEAT ENERGY* going either *IN* or *OUT*.

Melting — the rigid lattice breaks down

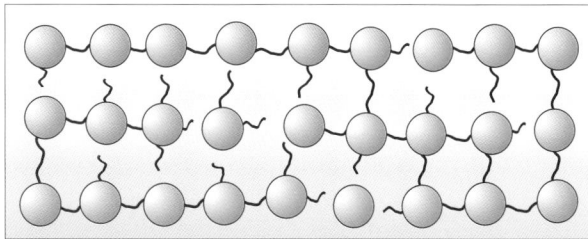

1) When a *SOLID* is *heated*, the heat energy goes to the *molecules*.
2) It makes them vibrate *more and more*.
3) Eventually the *strong forces* between the molecules (that hold them in the rigid lattice) are *overcome*, and the molecules start to move around. The solid has now *MELTED*.

Evaporation — the fastest molecules escape

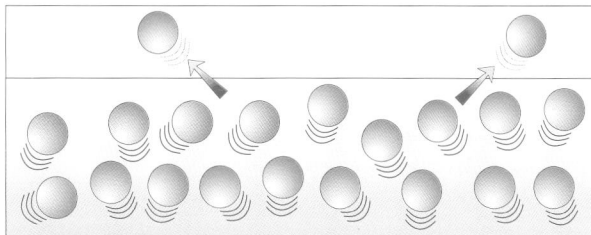

1) When a *LIQUID* is *heated*, the heat energy goes to the *molecules*, which makes them *move faster*.
2) Some molecules move faster than others.
3) Fast-moving molecules at the *surface* will *overcome* the forces of *attraction* from the other molecules and *escape*. This is *EVAPORATION*.

Boiling — all molecules are fast enough to escape

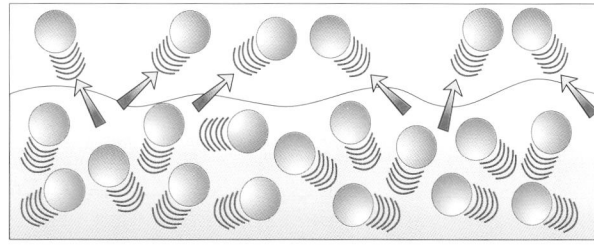

1) When the liquid gets *hot enough*, virtually *all* the molecules have enough *speed and energy* to overcome the forces and *escape* each other.
2) At this point big *bubbles* of *gas* form inside the liquid as the molecules break away from each other. This is *BOILING*.

Heating and Cooling Graphs Have Important Flat Spots

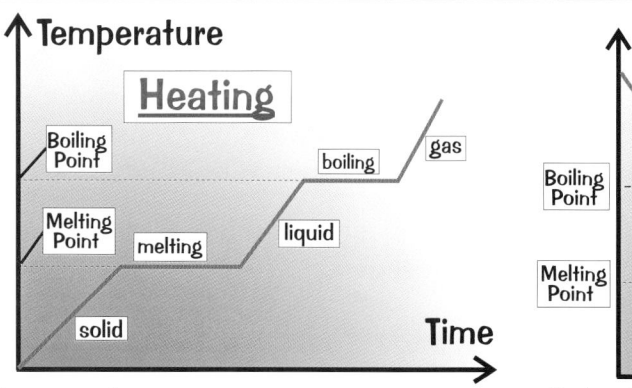

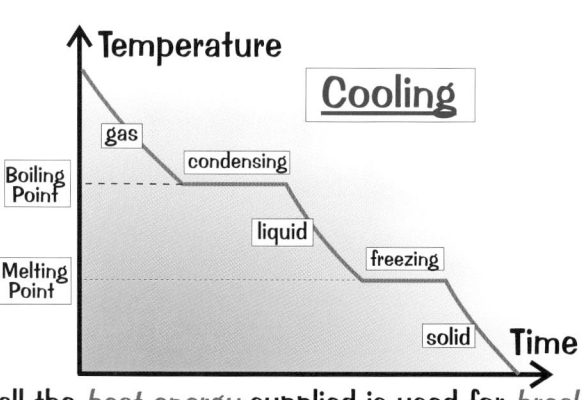

1) When a substance is *MELTING* or *BOILING*, all the *heat energy* supplied is used for *breaking bonds* rather than raising the temperature, hence the flat spots in the heating graph.
2) When a liquid is *cooled*, the graph for temperature will show a flat spot at the *freezing* point.
3) As the molecules *fuse* into a solid, *HEAT IS GIVEN OUT* as the bonds form, so the temperature *won't* go down until *all* the substance has turned to *solid*.

Revision — don't get all steamed up about it...

There are five diagrams and a total of 11 numbered points on this page. They wouldn't be there if you didn't need to learn them. *So learn them*. Then cover the page and scribble them all down. You have to realise this is the only way to really learn stuff properly. *And learn it you must*.

Brownian Motion and Diffusion

1) Brownian motion is the _jerky movement_ of _smoke_ particles, as seen through a microscope.
2) It's caused by _air_ molecules _bumping_ into the _smoke_ particles and knocking them about.
3) The smoke particles _reflect the light_ shone onto them — they're seen as _bright specks_.
4) Brownian motion can also be seen in _pollen grains in water_, looked at through a microscope.

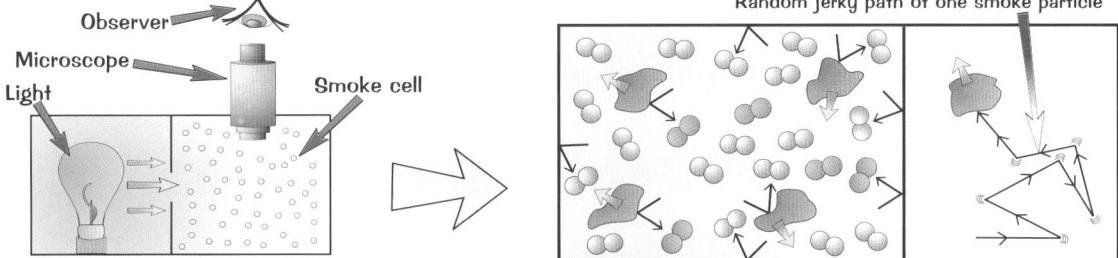

Three Gripping Diffusion Experiments

1) _DIFFUSION_ is when two gases or liquids merge together to form a mixture.
2) It happens because the _molecules_ in liquids and gases are in _constant rapid random motion_.
   Make sure you can explain what's happening in these three demonstrations.

1) Purple Potassium Manganate(VII) in water

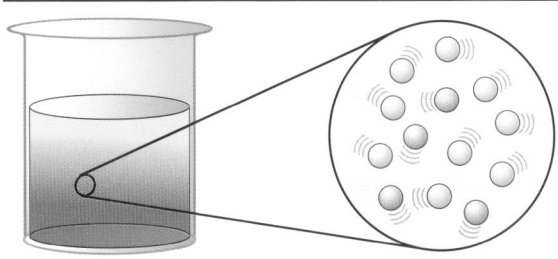

1) As it _dissolves_ into the water, the molecules of the purple potassium manganate(VII) gradually _diffuse_ through the _liquid_.
2) The constant _rapid random motion_ of all the molecules causes the purple colour to eventually spread _evenly_ through the whole liquid.

2) Good old Boring Brown Bromine in Air and in Vacuum

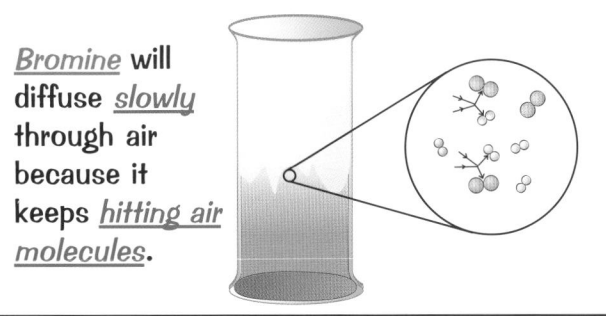

Bromine will diffuse _slowly_ through air because it keeps _hitting air molecules_.

But in a _vacuum_ bromine spreads _instantly_ because there are _no_ air molecules to get in the way.

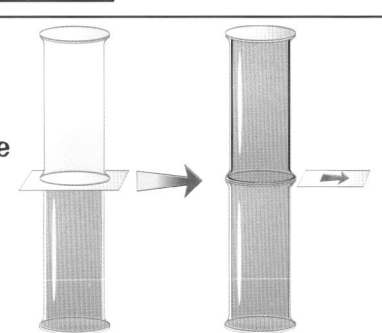

3) Diffusion of Hydrochloric Acid and Ammonia

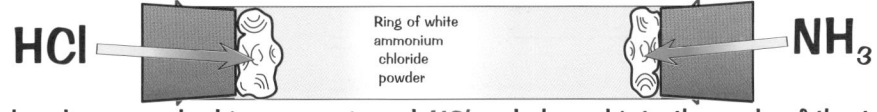

1) The cotton wool pads are soaked in _ammonia_ and _HCl_ and shoved into the ends of the tube.
2) The two liquids _evaporate_ and _diffuse_ through the air.
3) When they meet they form _ammonium chloride_, a white solid, visible inside the tube.
4) The _ring of white powder_ forms _nearer_ to the HCl end because the _ammonia_ travels _faster_.
5) This is because ammonia molecules are _lighter_, and lighter molecules always travel _faster_.

Diffusion — it's just a riot, don't you think...

When you think you know the whole page, _cover it up_ and scribble down all the diagrams together with the numbered points for each one. Turn back and _learn_ the bits you forgot. Then try again.

Atoms

The structure of atoms is real simple. I mean, gee, there's nothing to them. Just learn and enjoy.

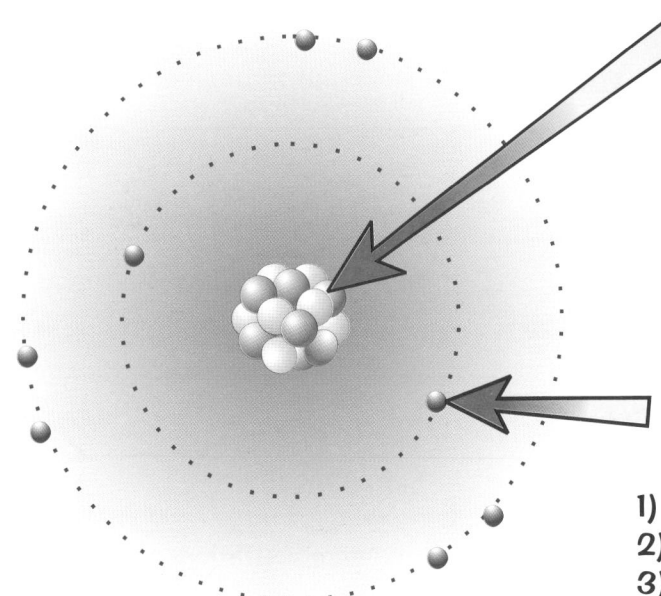

The Nucleus

1) It's in the _middle_ of the atom.
2) It contains _protons_ and _neutrons_.
3) It has a _positive charge_ because of the protons.
4) Almost the _whole_ mass of the atom is _concentrated_ in the nucleus.
5) But size-wise it's _tiny_ compared to the rest of the atom.

The Electrons

1) Move _around_ the nucleus.
2) They're _negatively charged_.
3) They're _tiny_, but they cover _a lot of space_.
4) The _volume_ their orbits occupy determines how big the atom is.
5) They have virtually _no_ mass.
6) They occupy _shells_ around the nucleus.
7) These shells explain _the whole of Chemistry_.

Atoms are _real tiny_, don't forget. They're _too small to see_, even with a microscope.

Number of Protons Equals Number of Electrons

1) Neutral atoms have _no charge_ overall.
2) The _charge_ on the electrons is the _same_ size as the charge on the _protons_ but _opposite_.
3) This means the _number_ of _protons_ always equals the _number_ of _electrons_ in a _neutral atom_.
4) If some electrons are _added or removed_, the atom becomes _charged_ and is then an _ION_.
5) The number of neutrons isn't fixed but is usually just a bit _higher_ than the number of protons.

Know Your Particles

PROTONS are _HEAVY_ and _POSITIVELY CHARGED_
NEUTRONS are _HEAVY_ and _NEUTRAL_
ELECTRONS are _Tiny_ and _NEGATIVELY CHARGED_

PARTICLE	MASS	CHARGE
Proton	1	+1
Neutron	1	0
Electron	$\frac{1}{2000}$	-1

Basic Atom facts — they don't take up much space...

This stuff on atoms should be permanently engraved in the minds of everyone.
I don't understand how people can get through the day without knowing this stuff, really I don't.
LEARN IT NOW, and watch as the Universe unfolds and reveals its timeless mysteries to you...

Proton Number and Mass Number

Come on. These are just *two simple numbers* for goodness' sake.
It just can't be that difficult to remember what they tell you about an atom.

THE MASS NUMBER

— Total of Protons and Neutrons

THE PROTON NUMBER

— Number of Protons
(sometimes called atomic number)

$^{23}_{11}Na$

POINTS TO NOTE

1) The *proton number* (or *atomic number*) tells you how many *protons* there are (oddly enough).
2) This *also* tells you how many *electrons* there are.
3) The *proton number* is what distinguishes one particular element from another.
4) To get the number of *neutrons* — just *subtract* the *proton number* from the *mass number*.
5) The *mass* number is always the *biggest* number. It tells you the relative mass of the atom.
6) The *mass* number is always roughly *double* the *proton* number.
7) Which means there's about the *same* number of protons as neutrons in any nucleus.

Isotopes are the same except for an extra neutron or two

A favourite trick Exam question: "Explain what is meant by the term *Isotope*"
The trick is that it's impossible to explain what one isotope is. Nice of them that isn't it!
You have to outsmart them and always start your answer *"ISOTOPES ARE...*
LEARN THE DEFINITION:

> *ISOTOPES ARE:* different atomic forms of the *same element*, which have
> the SAME number of PROTONS but a DIFFERENT number of NEUTRONS.

1) The upshot is: isotopes must have the *same* proton number but *different* mass numbers.
2) *If* they had *different* proton numbers, they'd be *different* elements altogether.
3) A very popular pair of isotopes are *carbon-12* and *carbon-14*.

Carbon-12

$^{12}_{6}C$

6 PROTONS
6 ELECTRONS
6 NEUTRONS

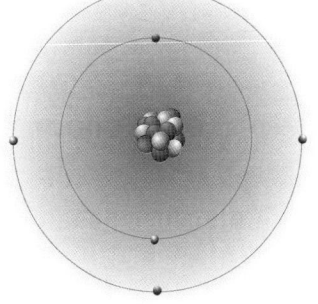

Carbon-14

$^{14}_{6}C$

6 PROTONS
6 ELECTRONS
8 NEUTRONS

The *number* of electrons decides the *chemistry* of the element. If the *proton number* is the same (that is, the *number of protons* is the same) then the *number of electrons* must be the same, so the *chemistry* is the same. The *different* number of *neutrons* in the nucleus *doesn't* affect the chemical behaviour *at all*.

Learn what those blinking numbers mean...

There really isn't that much information on this page — three definitions, a couple of diagrams and a dozen or so extra details.   All you gotta do is *READ IT*, *LEARN IT*, *COVER THE PAGE* and *SCRIBBLE IT ALL DOWN AGAIN*. Smile and enjoy.

6

Electron Shells

The fact that electrons occupy "shells" around the nucleus is what causes the whole of chemistry. Remember that, and watch how it applies to each bit of it. It's ace.

Electron Shell Rules:

1) Electrons always occupy *SHELLS* (sometimes called *ENERGY LEVELS*).
2) The *LOWEST* energy levels are *ALWAYS FILLED FIRST*.
3) Only *a certain number* of electrons are allowed in each shell:
   1st shell: 2   *2nd Shell:* 8   *3rd Shell:* 8
4) Atoms are much *HAPPIER* when they have *FULL electron shells*.
5) In most atoms the *OUTER SHELL* is *NOT FULL* and this makes the atom want to *REACT*.

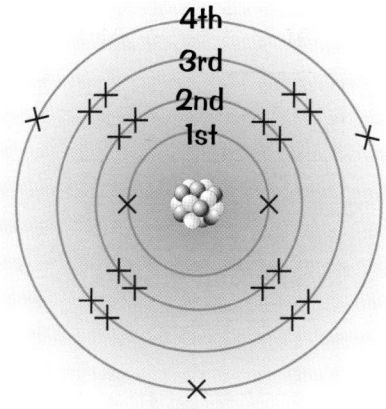

4th shell still filling

Working out Electron Configurations

You need to know the *electron configurations* for the first *20* elements. But they're not hard to work out. For a quick example, take Nitrogen. *Follow the steps...*

1) The periodic table (see below) tells us Nitrogen has *seven* protons... so it must have *seven* electrons.
2) Follow the 'Electron Shell Rules' above. The *first* shell can only take 2 electrons and the *second* shell can take a *maximum* of 8 electrons.

3) So the electron configuration for Nitrogen *must* be *2,5*. Easy peasy.
4) Now *you* try it for Argon.

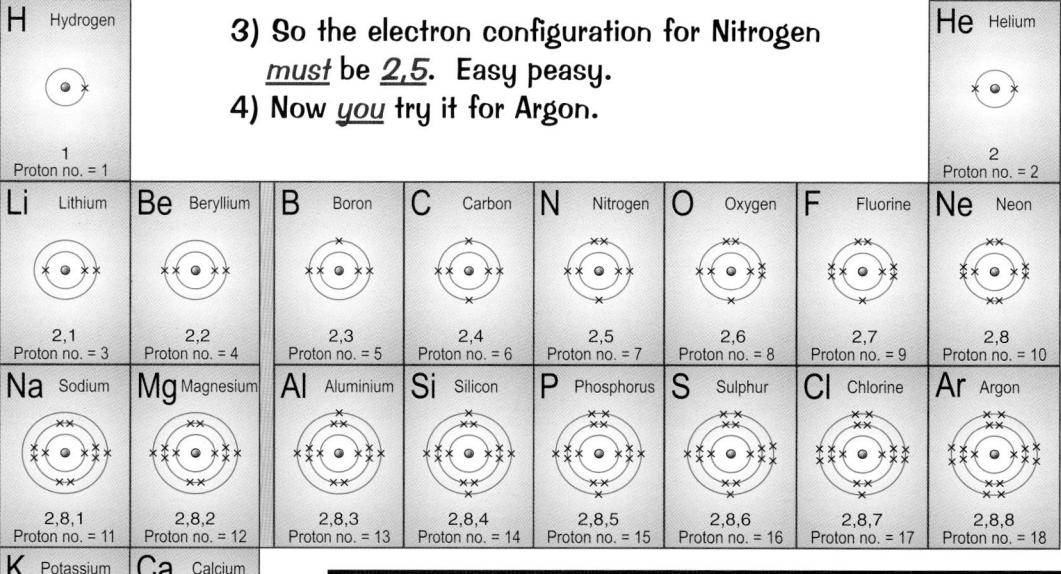

Answer... To calculate the electron configuration of argon, *follow the rules*. It's got 18 protons, so it *must* have 18 electrons. The first shell must have *2* electrons, the second shell must have *8*, and so the third shell must have *8* as well. It's as easy as *2,8,8*.

Electrons rule...

There's some *really important stuff* on this page and you *really do* need to *learn all of it*. Once you have, it'll make all of the rest of the stuff in this book an awful lot *easier*. Practise calculating *electron configurations* and drawing *electron shell* diagrams.

Elements, Compounds & Mixtures

You'd better be sure you know the _subtle difference_ between these.

Elements consist of one type of atom only

Quite a lot of everyday substances are _elements_:

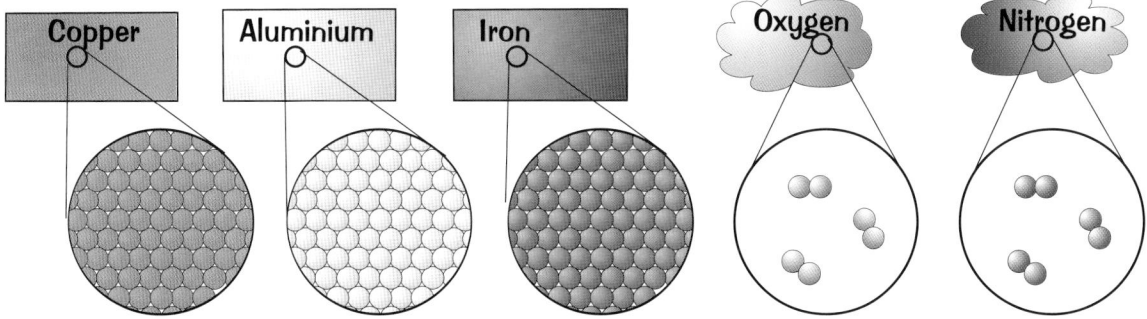

Mixtures _are easily separated_

1) _Air_ is a _mixture_ of gases.
   The oxygen, nitrogen, argon and carbon dioxide can all be _separated_ out quite _easily_.
2) There is _no chemical bond_ between the different parts of a mixture.
3) The _properties_ of a mixture are just a mixture of the properties of the _separate parts_.
4) A mixture of _iron powder_ and _sulphur powder_ will show the properties of _both iron and sulphur_. It will contain grey magnetic bits of iron and bright yellow bits of sulphur.

Air is a
mixture
of gases

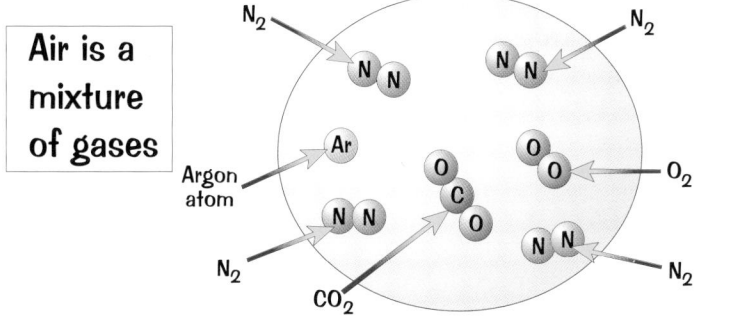

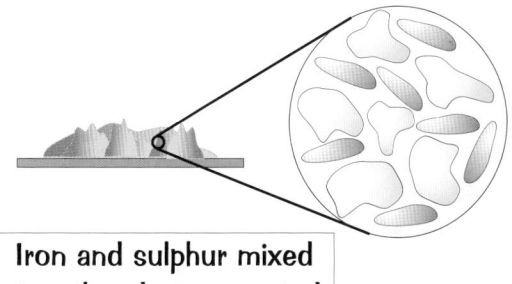

Iron and sulphur mixed
together, but unreacted.

Compounds _are chemically bonded_

1) Carbon dioxide is a _compound_ formed from a _chemical reaction_ between carbon and oxygen.
2) It's _very difficult_ to _separate_ the two original elements out again.
3) The _properties_ of a compound are _totally different_ from the properties of the _original elements_.
4) If iron and sulphur react to form _iron sulphide_, the compound formed is a _grey solid lump_, and doesn't behave _anything like_ either iron or sulphur.

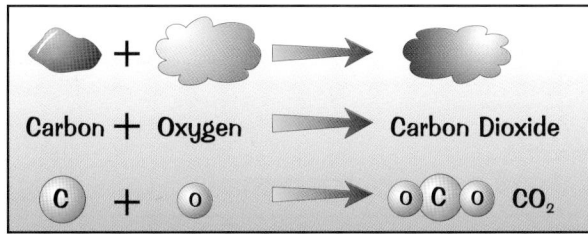

Carbon + Oxygen ⟶ Carbon Dioxide

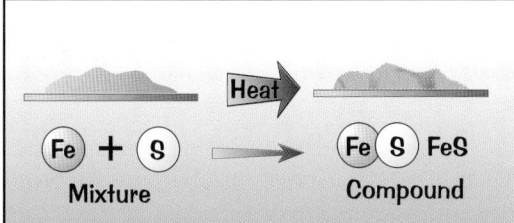

Don't mix these up — it'll only compound your problems...

Elements, mixtures and compounds. To most people they sound like basically the same thing.
_Ha!_ Not to GCSE Examiners they don't, pal! You make mighty sure you remember their
different names and the differences between them. _Just more easy marks to be won or lost._

Ionic Bonding

Ionic Bonding — Swapping Electrons

In _IONIC BONDING_, atoms _lose or gain electrons_ to form _charged particles_ (ions) which are then _strongly attracted_ to one another, (the attraction of opposite charges, + and –).

A shell with just one electron is well keen to get rid...

All the atoms over at the _left hand side_ of the periodic table, such as _sodium, potassium, calcium_ etc. have just _one or two electrons_ in their outer shell. And basically they're _pretty keen to get shot of them_, because then they'll only have _full shells_ left, which is how they _like_ it. So given half a chance they do get rid, and that leaves the atom as an _ION_ instead. Now ions aren't the kind of things that sit around quietly watching the world go by. They tend to _leap_ at the first passing ion with an _opposite charge_ and stick to it like glue.

A nearly full shell is well keen to get that extra electron...

On the _other side_ of the periodic table, the elements in _Group Six_ and _Group Seven_, such as _oxygen_ and _chlorine_ have outer shells which are _nearly full_. They're obviously pretty keen to _gain_ that _extra one or two electrons_ to fill the shell up. When they do of course they become _IONS_, you know, not the kind of things to sit around, and before you know it, _POP_, they've latched onto the atom (ion) that gave up the electron a moment earlier. The reaction of sodium and chlorine is a _classic case_:

The _sodium_ atom _gives up_ its _outer electron_ and becomes an Na$^+$ ion.

The _chlorine_ atom _picks up_ the _spare electron_ and becomes a Cl$^-$ ion.

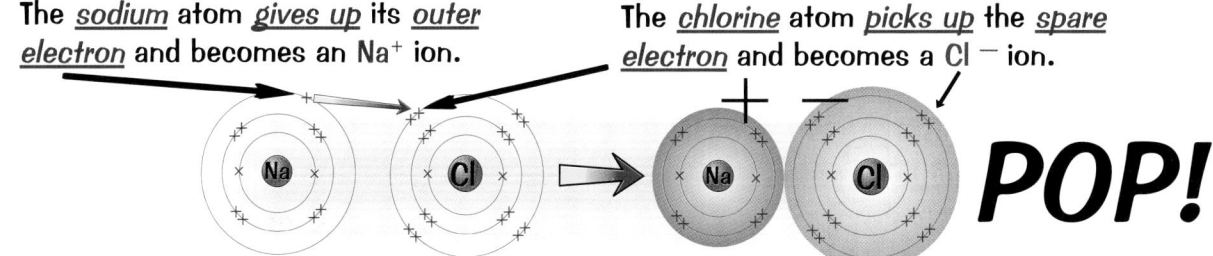

POP!

Giant Ionic Structures don't melt easily, but when they do...

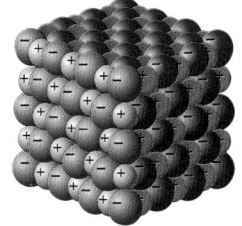
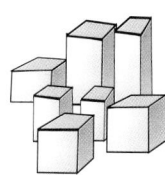

1) _Ionic bonds_ always produce _giant ionic structures_.
2) The ions form a _closely packed_ regular lattice arrangement.
3) There are _very strong_ chemical bonds between _all_ the ions.
4) A single crystal of salt is _one giant ionic lattice_, which is why salt crystals tend to be cuboid in shape.

1) _They have High melting points and boiling points_
due to the _very strong_ chemical bonds between _all the ions_ in the giant structure.

2) _They Dissolve to form solutions that conduct electricity_
When dissolved the ions _separate_ and are all _free to move_ in the solution, so obviously they'll _carry electric current_.

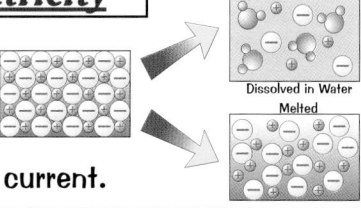
Dissolved in Water
Melted

3) _They Conduct electricity when molten_
When it _melts_, the ions are _free to move_ and they'll carry electric current.

Full Shells — it's the name of the game, pal...

Make sure you know exactly _how_ and _why_ ionic bonds are formed. There's quite a lot of words on this page but only to hammer home _three basic points_: 1) Ionic bonds involve _swapping_ electrons 2) Some atoms like to _lose_ them, some like to _gain_ them 3) Ionic bonds lead to the formation of giant ionic structures. Learn _all_ the features of giant ionic structures.

Electron Shells and Ions

Simple Ions — Groups 1 & 2 and 6 & 7

1) Remember, atoms that have _lost_ or _gained_ an electron (or electrons) are _ions_.
2) The elements that most readily form ions are those in Groups 1, 2, 6, and 7.
3) _Group 1 and 2 elements_ are _metals_ and they _lose_ electrons to form _+ve ions_ or _cations_.
4) _Group 6 and 7 elements_ are _non-metals_. They _gain_ electrons to form _–ve ions_ or _anions_.
5) Make sure you know these easy ones:

CATIONS		ANIONS	
Gr I	**Gr II**	**Gr VI**	**Gr VII**
Li^+	Be^{2+}	O^{2-}	F^-
Na^+	Mg^{2+}	Cl^-	
K^+	Ca^{2+}		

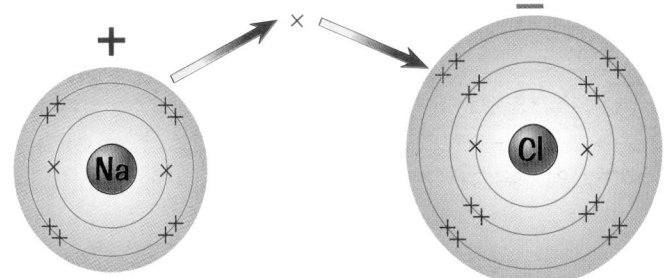

6) When any of the above elements _react together_, they form _ionic bonds_.
7) Only elements at _opposite sides_ of the periodic table will form ionic bonds, e.g. Na and Cl, where one of them becomes a _CATION_ (+ve) and one becomes an _ANION_ (–ve).

> Remember, the + and – charges we talk about, e.g. Na^+ for sodium, just tell you _what type of ion the atom WILL FORM_ in a chemical reaction. In sodium _metal_ there are _only neutral sodium atoms, Na_. The Na^+ ions _will only appear_ if the sodium metal _reacts_ with something like water or chlorine.

Electronic structure of some simple ions

A useful way of representing ions is by specifying the _ion's name_, followed by its _electron configuration_ and the _charge_ on the ion. For example, the electronic structure of the sodium ion Na^+ can be represented by $[2,8]^+$. That's the electron configuration followed by the charge on the ion. Simple enough. A few _ions_ and the _ionic compounds_ they form are shown below.

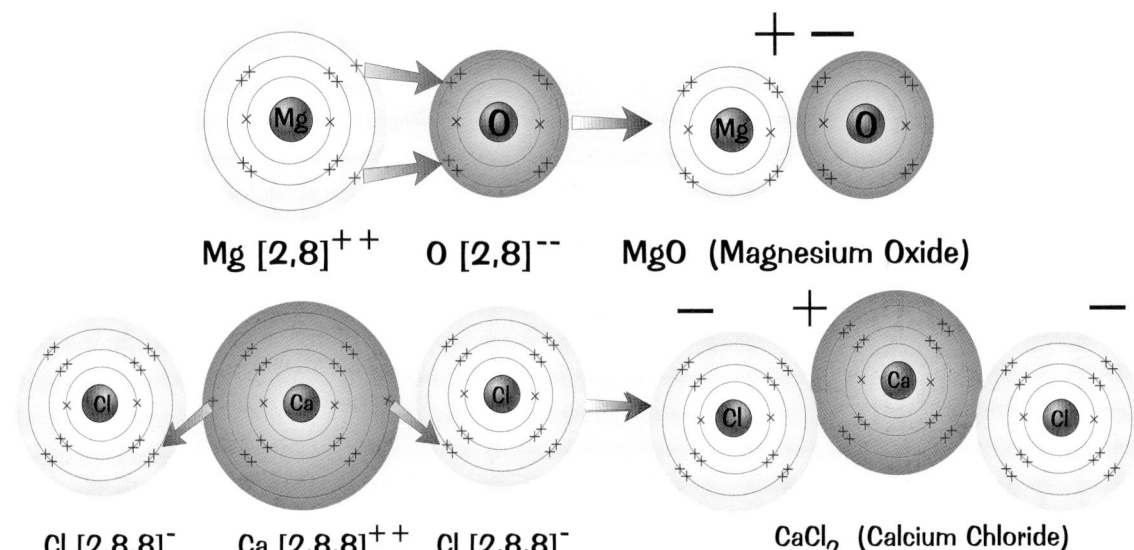

Mg $[2,8]^{++}$ O $[2,8]^{--}$ MgO (Magnesium Oxide)

Cl $[2,8,8]^-$ Ca $[2,8,8]^{++}$ Cl $[2,8,8]^-$ $CaCl_2$ (Calcium Chloride)

Simple ions — looks simple enough to me...

Yet again, more stuff you've _got_ to know. _LEARN_ which atoms form 1+, 1-, 2+ and 2- ions, and why. You need to know how to represent ions _both_ in [x,y] notation _and_ by diagrams. When you think you've got it, _cover the page_ and start scribbling to see what you really know. Then look back, _learn the bits you missed_, and _try again_. And again.

Covalent Bonding

Covalent Bonds — Sharing Electrons

1) Sometimes atoms prefer to make _COVALENT BONDS_ by _sharing_ electrons with other atoms.
2) This way _both_ atoms feel that they have a _full outer shell_, and that makes them happy.
3) Each _covalent bond_ provides one _extra_ shared electron for each atom.
4) Each atom involved has to make _enough_ covalent bonds to _fill up_ its outer shell.

5) _LEARN_ these _FIVE IMPORTANT EXAMPLES_:

1) Hydrogen Gas, H_2

Hydrogen atoms have just one electron. They _only need one more_ to complete the first shell...

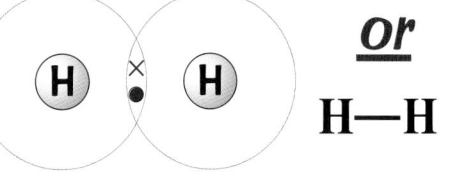

_or_

H—H

...so they often form _single covalent bonds_ to achieve this.

2) Hydrogen Chloride HCl

This is very similar to H_2. Again, both atoms _only need one more electron_ to complete their outer shells.

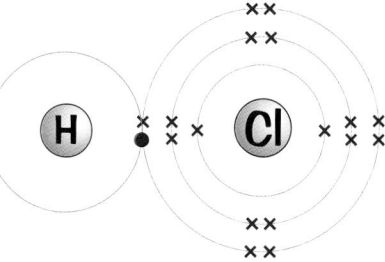

_or_   H—Cl

3) Ammonia, NH_3

Nitrogen has _five_ outer electrons...

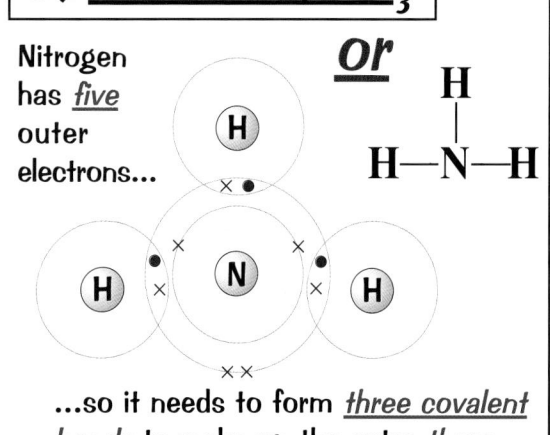

_or_

H—N—H
|
H

...so it needs to form _three covalent bonds_ to make up the extra _three_ electrons needed.

4) Methane, CH_4

Carbon has _four outer electrons_, which is a _half full_ shell.

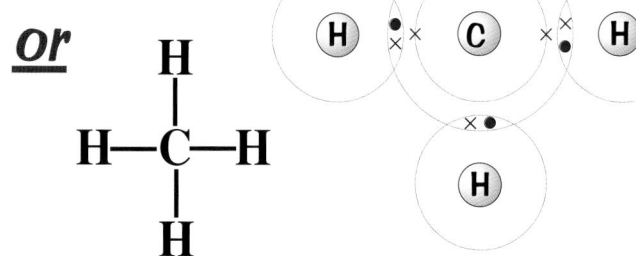

_or_

H
|
H—C—H
|
H

To become a 4+ or a 4− ion is hard work so it forms _four covalent bonds_ to make up its outer shell.

5) Water, H_2O

_or_

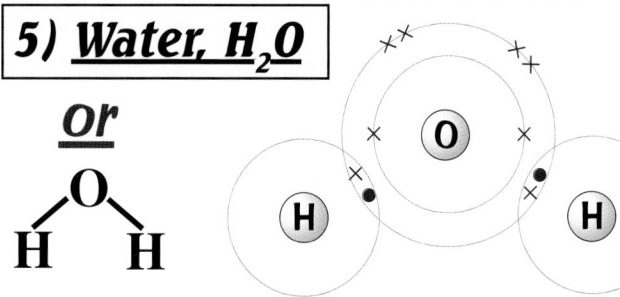

O
/ \
H   H

The _oxygen_ atom has _six_ outer electrons. Sometimes it forms _ionic_ bonds by _taking_ two electrons to complete the outer shell. However it will also cheerfully form _covalent bonds_ and _SHARE_ two electrons instead, as in the case of _water molecules_, where it _shares_ electrons with the H atoms.

Full Shells — you just can't beat them...

LEARN the four numbered points about covalent bonds and the five examples.
Then turn over and scribble it all down again. Make sure you can draw all five molecules and explain exactly why they form the bonds that they do. _All from memory of course._

Covalent Substances: Two Kinds

Substances formed from *covalent bonds* can either be *simple molecules* or *giant structures*.

Simple Molecular Substances

1) The atoms form *very strong* covalent bonds to form *small* molecules of several atoms.
2) By contrast, the forces of attraction *between* these molecules are *very weak*.
3) The result of these feeble *inter-molecular forces* is that the *melting-* and *boiling-points* are *very low*, because the molecules are *easily parted* from each other.
4) Most molecular substances are *gases or liquids* at room temperature.
5) Molecular substances *don't conduct electricity*, simply because there are *no ions*.
6) They *don't dissolve in water*, usually.
7) You can usually tell a molecular substance just from its *physical state*, which is always kinda '*mushy*' — i.e. *liquid* or *gas* or an *easily-melted solid*.

Very weak inter-molecular forces

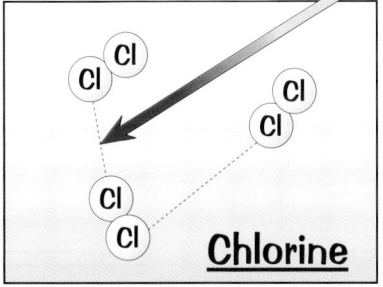
Chlorine

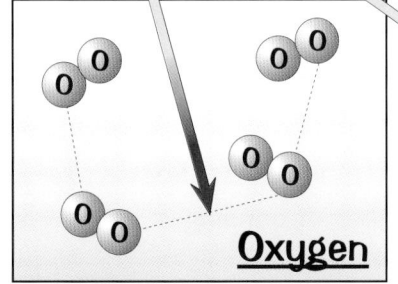
Oxygen

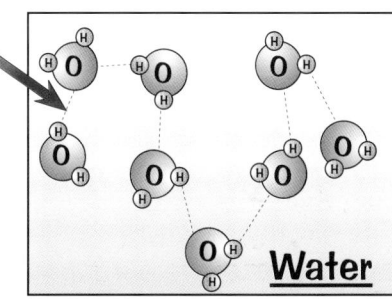
Water

Giant Covalent Structures

1) These are similar to giant ionic structures except that there are *no charged ions*.
2) *All* the atoms are *bonded* to *each other* by *strong* covalent bonds.
3) They have *very high* melting and boiling points.
4) They *don't conduct electricity* — not even when *molten*.
5) They're usually *insoluble* in water.
6) The *main examples* are *Diamond* and *Graphite* which are both made only from *carbon atoms*.

Diamond

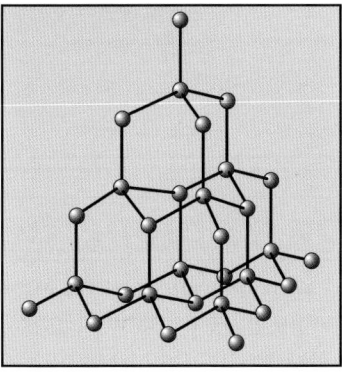

Each carbon atom forms *four covalent bonds* in a *very rigid* giant covalent structure.

Graphite

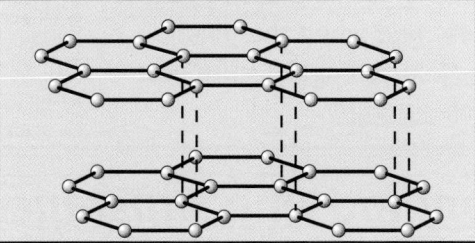

Each carbon atom only forms *three covalent bonds*, creating *layers* which are free to *slide over each other*, and leaving *free electrons*, so graphite is the only *non-metal* which *conducts electricity*.

Silicon Dioxide

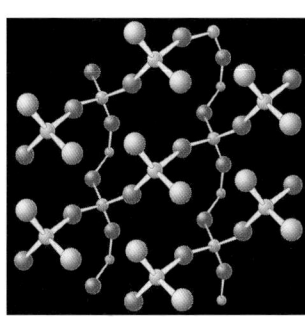

Sometimes called *silica*, this is what *sand* is made of.
Each grain of sand is *one giant structure* of silicon and oxygen.

Come on — pull yourself together...

There are two types of covalently bonded substances — and they're totally different. Make sure you know all the details about them and the examples too. *This is real basic stuff* — just easy marks to be won... or lost. *Cover the page* and see how many marks you're gonna *WIN*.

Metallic and Plastic structures

Metal Properties are all due to the Sea of Free Electrons

1) *Metals* also consist of a *giant structure*.
2) *Metallic bonds* involve the all-important '*free electrons*', which produce *all* the properties of metals. These free electrons come from the *outer shell* of *every* metal atom in the structure.
3) These electrons are *free to move* and so metals conduct *heat and electricity*.
4) These electrons also *hold* the atoms together in a regular structure.
5) They also allow the atoms to *slide* over each other causing metals to be *malleable*.

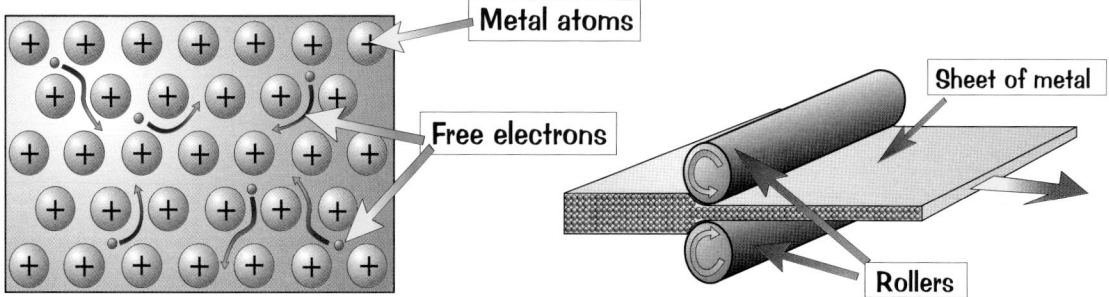

Metal atoms

Free electrons

Sheet of metal

Rollers

Thermosoftening and Thermosetting Plastics

The diagrams show the different types of bonding in these two *different types* of plastic.

In a *THERMOSOFTENING PLASTIC*, the long chains have no '*cross links*' so, as the plastic is heated, the long chains *loosen* their weak grip on their neighbours and the plastic goes *soft*. This will happen *every time* the plastic is heated. As soon as it *cools* the long chains *attract* each other again, the weak bonds *reform*, and the plastic becomes more *rigid* again.

In a *THERMOSETTING PLASTIC*, there are no cross-bonds *initially*, and the first time the plastic is heated it goes soft. However, the covalent bond *crosslinks* then *form* between the long-chain polymers, and when the plastic sets, it sets for good and *will not* soften again. The new crosslinks make the plastic much *stronger*.

Thermosoftening Plastic

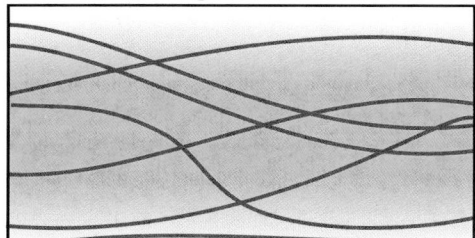

Thermosetting Plastic

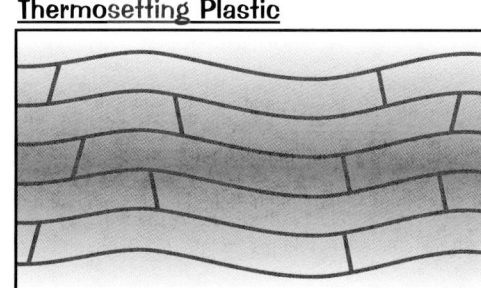

Identifying the bonding in a substance by its properties

If you've learnt the properties of the *six types* of substance properly, together with their *names* of course, then you should be able to easily *identify* most substances just by the way they *behave* as either: *ionic*, *giant-covalent*, *molecular*, *metallic*, *thermosoftening* or *thermosetting*. The way they're likely to test you in the Exam is by describing the *physical properties* of a substance and asking you to decide *which type of bonding* it has and therefore what type of material it is. If you know your onions you'll have no trouble at all. If not, you're gonna struggle.

Bonding — where would we all be without it...

A good approach here is the *mini-essay method*, where you just write down everything you can about each section, and then look back to see what you missed. This is much better than trying to remember the numbered points in the right order. *Try it for all six types of bonding*.

Tests and Hazard Symbols

You need to know these *FIVE EASY LAB TESTS:*

1) *Chlorine bleaches damp litmus paper*

(i.e. it *turns it white*).

2) *Oxygen relights a glowing splint*

The standard test for *oxygen* is that *it relights a glowing splint*.

3) *Carbon dioxide turns limewater milky*

Carbon dioxide can be detected by the way it *turns limewater cloudy* when it's bubbled through it.

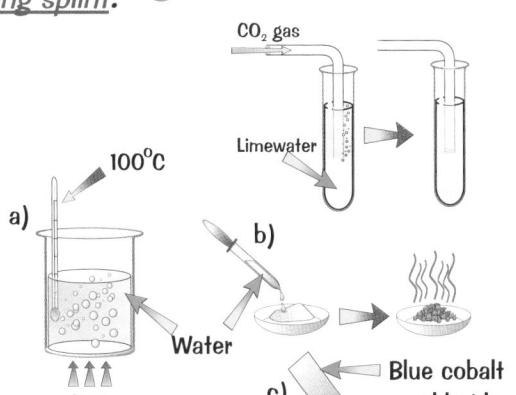

4) *The three lab tests for Water*

Water can be detected in three ways:
a) by its *boiling point of 100°C*
b) by *turning white anhydrous copper sulphate* to *blue hydrated copper sulphate* (and getting hot)
c) by turning *anhydrous cobalt chloride paper* from *blue* to *pink*.

5) *Lab test for Hydrogen — the notorious "Squeaky pop"*

Just bring *a lighted splint* near the gas with air around. If it's hydrogen it'll make a *'squeaky pop'* as it burns with the oxygen in the air to form H_2O.

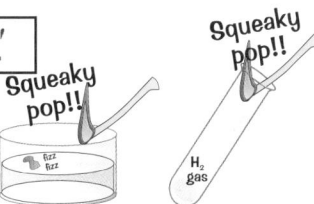

Hazard Symbols

Oxidising
Provides oxygen which allows other materials to *burn more fiercely*.
EXAMPLE: Liquid Oxygen.

Harmful
Similar to toxic but *not quite as dangerous*.
EXAMPLE: Petrol, meths.

Highly Flammable
Catches fire easily.
EXAMPLE: Petrol.

Corrosive
Attacks and destroys living tissues, including eyes and skin.
EXAMPLE: Sulphuric acid.

Toxic
Can cause death either by swallowing, breathing in, or absorption through the skin. *EXAMPLE:* Cyanide.

Irritant
Not corrosive but *can cause reddening or blistering of the skin*.
EXAMPLES: Bleach, children, etc.

Learn the Five Lab Tests — easy as squeaky pop...

This is pretty basic stuff, but people still lose marks in the Exam because they don't make sure to learn all the little details really thoroughly. That's true for just about everything in this book. It's no good just letting your eyes drift lazily across the page and thinking "Oh yeah, I know all that stuff". You've gotta really make sure you *do* know it all. *And there's only one way to do that* — so do it now.

Revision Summary for Section One

These certainly aren't the easiest questions you're going to come across. That's because they test what you know without giving you any clues. At first you might think they're impossibly difficult. Eventually you'll realise that they simply test whether you've learnt the stuff or not. If you're struggling to answer these then you need to do some serious learning.

1) What are the three states of matter?
2) Describe the bonding and atom spacing in all three states.
3) Describe the physical properties of each of these three states of matter.
4) What are the three ways of changing between the three states of matter?
5) Explain what goes on in all three processes, in terms of bonds and heat energy.
6) Sketch a heating graph and a cooling graph, with lots of labels.
7) Explain why these graphs have flat spots.
8) Sketch three gripping diffusion experiments and explain what happens in them.
9) Sketch an atom. Give five details about the nucleus and five details about the electrons.
10) What are the three particles found in an atom?
11) Do a table showing their relative masses and charges.
12) How do the number of these particles compare to each other in a neutral atom?
13) What do the mass number and proton number represent?
14) Explain what an isotope is. (!) Give a well-known example.
15) List five facts (or "Rules") about electron shells.
16) Calculate the electron configuration for each of the following elements: $^{4}_{2}He$, $^{12}_{6}C$, $^{31}_{15}P$, $^{39}_{19}K$.
17) For the four elements in the previous question, draw diagrams of the electron shells.
18) What is the difference between elements, mixtures and compounds?
19) Give three examples for each of elements, mixtures and compounds.
20) What is ionic bonding? Which kind of atoms like to do ionic bonding?
21) Why do atoms want to form ionic bonds anyway?
22) Draw a diagram of a giant ionic lattice and give three features of giant ionic structures.
23) What kind of ions are formed by elements in Groups I, II, and those in Groups VI and VII?
24) List the three main properties of ionic compounds.
25) Which atoms form 1+, 1-, 2+ and 2- ions?
26) Describe the electronic structure of the ions in these compounds: NaCl, MgO and $CaCl_2$.
27) Draw diagrams illustrating exactly how the ionic compounds MgO and $CaCl_2$ form.
28) What is covalent bonding? Which kind of atoms tend to do covalent bonding?
29) Why do some atoms do covalent bonding instead of ionic bonding?
30) Describe and draw diagrams to illustrate the bonding in: H_2, HCl, NH_3, CH_4 and H_2O.
31) Draw simplified diagrams (not showing the electrons) of the five substances described above.
32) What are the two types of covalent substances? Give three examples of each type.
33) Give three physical properties for each of the two types of covalent substance.
34) Explain how the bonding in each type of covalent substance causes its physical properties.
35) Why can graphite sometimes be used as a lubricant? Why is it used for pencil 'leads'?
36) Diamond and sand are both very hard. How come?
37) What is special about the bonding in metals?
38) What enables metals to conduct heat and electricity?
39) List the three main properties of metals and explain how the metallic bonding causes them.
40) Describe the difference between thermosoftening and thermosetting plastics.
41) Write a mini essay, describing the structure and bonding of all six types of substance.
42) Give full details of the lab tests for: Chlorine, oxygen, carbon dioxide, water (3), hydrogen.
43) Sketch the six Hazard Symbols, explain what they mean, and give an example for each.

Crude Oil

Fossil Fuels were formed from dead plants and animals

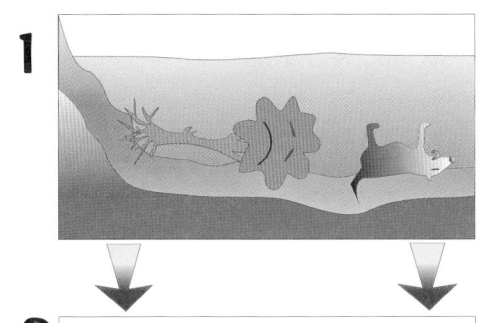

1

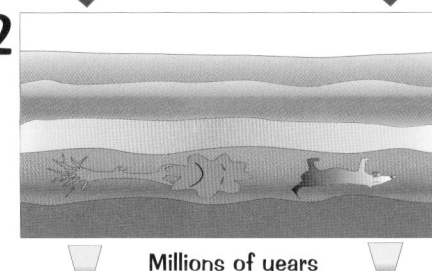

2

Millions of years
of heat and pressure

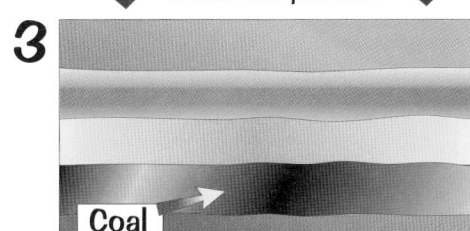

3

Coal

1) _Fossil fuels_ have formed over _millions_ of years.

2) Plants and animals _died_ and were _immediately_ covered by _sediment_ in _seas_ or _swamps_.

3) This _stopped_ them decaying.

4) Further layers of sediment buried the plant and animal remains _deeper_ and _deeper_.

5) After _millions_ of years of _pressure and heat_ (90°C to 120°C), in an environment with no air, these remains turned into _COAL_, _OIL_ and _NATURAL GAS_.

6) _Coal_ comes mainly from _dead plants_, like trees, falling into swamps.

7) _Oil_ and _gas_ occur _together_ and were formed from _both_ _plants_ and _animals_ being buried.

8) Fossil fuels are made from the _'fossil'_ remains of plants and animals. Hence the name.

9) When we burn fossil fuels we're using the _sun's energy_ that has been stored as _chemical energy_ underground for _millions_ of years.

Extracting Oil and Gas is pretty easy — once you find it

1) Coal is _solid_ so it just sits tight, waiting to be dug up.

2) _Oil and gas_ on the other hand tend to _move_.

3) They seep _upwards_ through _porous_ rocks such as sandstone, and _may_ reach the surface.

4) If they do, the gas _escapes_ and the oil forms pools of _black sludge_.

5) Once people realised how _useful_ the sludge was they started _drilling_ down for it.

6) Oil and gas can form into large _pockets_ if it gets _trapped_ under a layer of _non-porous_ rock.

7) Experts guess where there might be oil and they drill down.

8) When they strike lucky, the oil is _usually_ under pressure and comes up of its own accord.

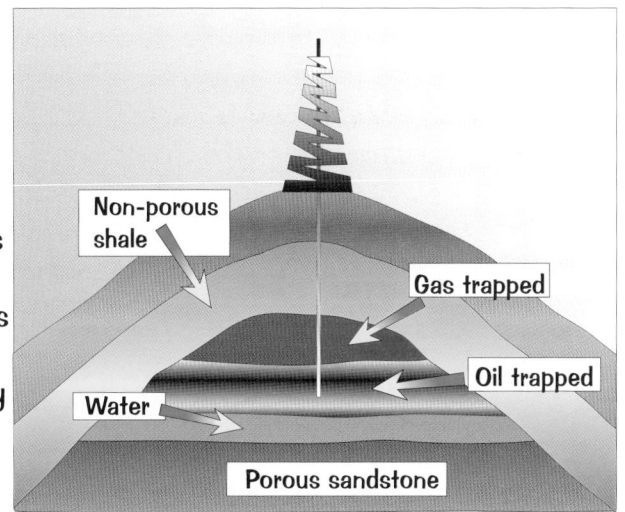

Non-porous shale

Gas trapped

Oil trapped

Water

Porous sandstone

Revising for oil — you know the drill...

There are two sections on this page, with a total of 17 important points. You do realise they _won't_ ask you what colour oil is or whether it grows on trees or comes out of the ground, etc. No, they'll ask you about these more technical details, _so make sure you learn them all_.

Distillation of Crude Oil

1) *Crude oil* is a mixture of different sized <u>hydrocarbon</u> molecules.
2) <u>Hydrocarbons</u> are basically <u>fuels</u> such as petrol and diesel.
3) The <u>bigger</u> and <u>longer</u> the molecules, the <u>less runny</u> the hydrocarbon (fuel) is.
4) <u>Fractional distillation</u> splits crude oil up into its separate <u>fractions</u>.
5) The <u>shorter the molecules</u>, the <u>lower the temperature</u> at which that fraction <u>condenses</u>.

Crude Oil is Split into Separate Hydrocarbons (fuels)

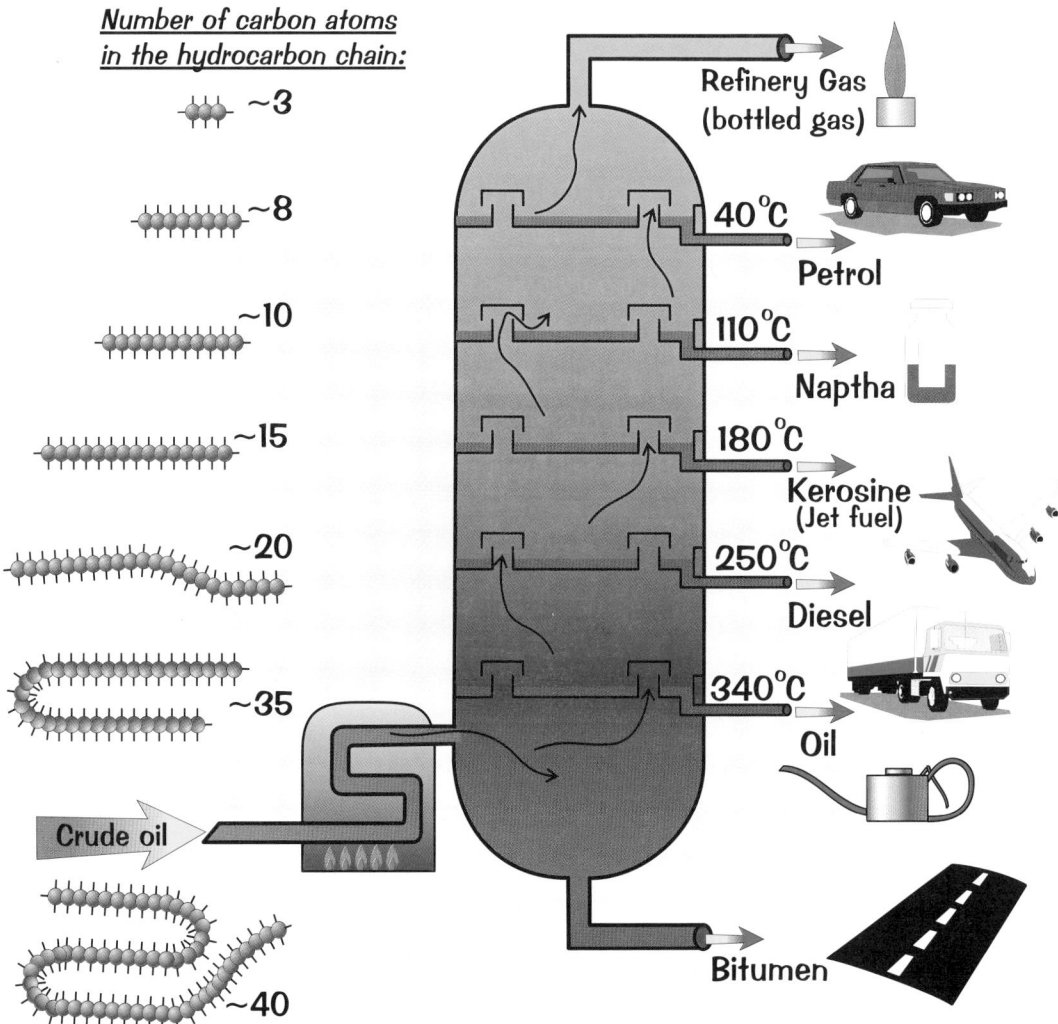

Number of carbon atoms in the hydrocarbon chain:

~3
~8
~10
~15
~20
~35
~40

Crude oil

Refinery Gas (bottled gas)

40°C Petrol

110°C Naptha

180°C Kerosine (Jet fuel)

250°C Diesel

340°C Oil

Bitumen

The <u>fractionating column</u> works continuously, with heated crude oil piped in <u>at the bottom</u> and the various <u>fractions</u> being constantly tapped off at the different levels where they <u>condense</u>.

Crude oil is a very big part of modern life

1) It provides the <u>fuel</u> for most modern transport.
2) It also provides the <u>raw material</u> for making various <u>chemicals</u> including <u>PLASTICS</u>. Plastics are just ace, of course. The world without plastics? Why, it would be the end of civilisation as we know it...

OK, so it's an easy page — don't let it go to your head...

A typical question would show a fractionating column and ask you which bit you'd expect petrol or diesel to come out of, or ask you how long the carbon chain of diesel is, or ask you to give the main uses of crude oil. So make sure you know <u>*ALL*</u> the details. When you think you do, <u>cover up the page</u> and <u>scribble down</u> all the details including the diagram. <u>*Then try again*</u>.

Using Hydrocarbons

Hydrocarbons are long chain molecules

As the *SIZE* of the hydrocarbon molecule *INCREASES*:

1) The *BOILING POINT* increases

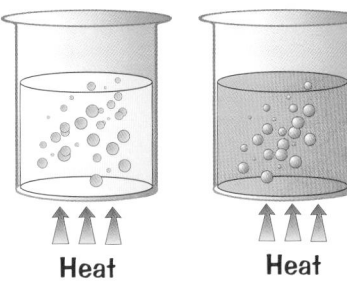

Heat   Heat

2) It gets *LESS FLAMMABLE*

(doesn't set fire so easy)

3) It gets *MORE VISCOUS*

(doesn't flow so easy)

4) It gets *LESS VOLATILE*

(i.e. doesn't evaporate so easily)

The *vapours* of the more *volatile* hydrocarbons are *very flammable* and pose a serious *fire risk*.
So don't smoke at the petrol station. (In fact, don't smoke at all, it's stupid.)

Complete combustion of Hydrocarbons is safe

The complete combustion of any hydrocarbon in oxygen will produce only
carbon dioxide and *water* as waste products, which are both quite *clean* and *non poisonous*.

hydrocarbon + oxygen → carbon dioxide + water (+ energy)

Many *gas room heaters* release these *waste gases* into the room, which is perfectly OK.
As long as the gas heater is working properly and the room is well ventilated there's
no problem. When there's *plenty of oxygen* the gas burns with a *clean blue flame*.

But Incomplete combustion of Hydrocarbons is NOT safe

If there isn't enough oxygen the combustion will be *INCOMPLETE*.
This gives *carbon monoxide* and *carbon* as waste products,
and produces a *smoky yellow flame*:

hydrocarbon + oxygen → CO_2 + H_2O + carbon monoxide + carbon (+ energy)

The *carbon monoxide* is a *colourless*, *odourless* and *poisonous* gas and it's *very dangerous*.
Every year people are *killed* while they sleep due to *faulty* gas fires and boilers filling the room
with *deadly* carbon monoxide, CO, and nobody realising. The black carbon given off produces
sooty marks and is a *clue* that the fuel is *not* burning fully.

The one burning question is... have you learnt it all...

Four features of hydrocarbons which change with increasing chain length, and the details for
complete and incomplete combustion. *All worth juicy marks in the Exam*. So learn and enjoy.

Cracking Hydrocarbons

Cracking — splitting up long chain hydrocarbons

1) *LONG CHAIN* hydrocarbons form *thick* gloopy liquids like *tar* which aren't all that useful.

2) The process called *cracking* turns them into *SHORTER* molecules which are *much* more useful.

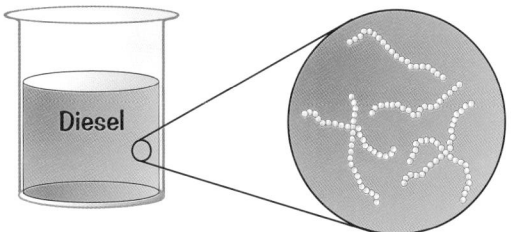 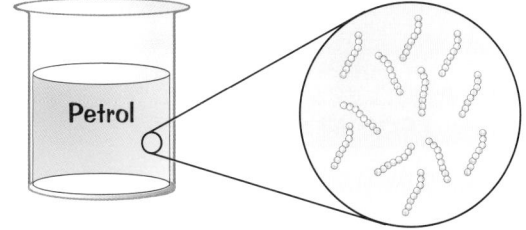

3) *CRACKING* is a form of *thermal decomposition*, which just means *breaking* molecules down into *simpler* molecules by *heating* them.

4) A lot of the longer molecules produced from fractional distillation are *cracked* into smaller ones because there's *more demand* for products like *petrol* and *paraffin* (jet fuel) than for diesel or lubricating oil.

5) More importantly, cracking produces *extra alkenes* which are needed for making *plastics*.

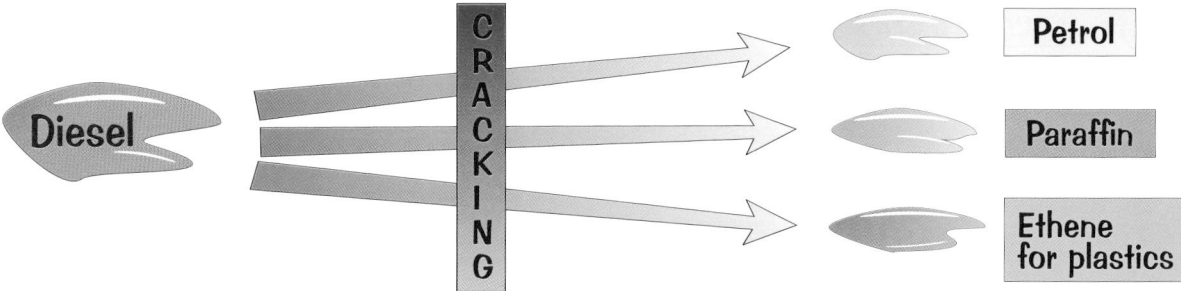

Industrial Conditions for Cracking: *hot, plus a catalyst*

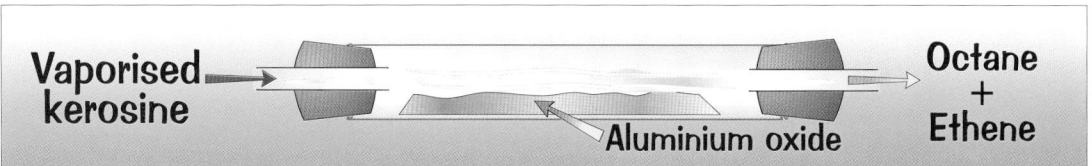

1) *Vaporised hydrocarbons* are passed over a *powdered catalyst* at about *400°C – 700°C*.

2) *Aluminium oxide* is the catalyst used.
   The *long chain* molecules *split apart* or "crack" on the *surface* of the bits of catalyst.

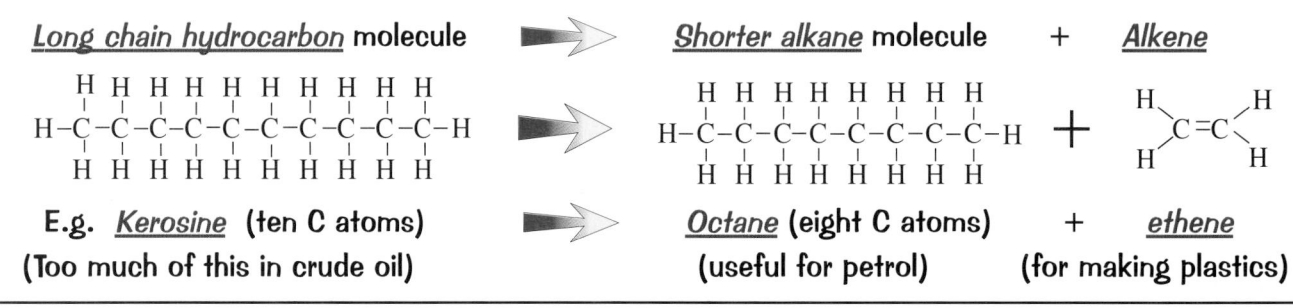

Long chain hydrocarbon molecule	➤	*Shorter alkane* molecule	+	*Alkene*
E.g. *Kerosine* (ten C atoms)	➤	*Octane* (eight C atoms)	+	*ethene*
(Too much of this in crude oil)		(useful for petrol)		(for making plastics)

Chemistry — what a cracking subject it is...

Five details about the whys and wherefores, two details of the industrial conditions and a specific example showing typical products: a shorter chain alkane and an alkene. *LEARN IT ALL.*

Alkanes and Alkenes

Crude oil contains both _alkanes_ and _alkenes_. Know the differences between them.

ALKANES have all C–C SINGLE bonds

Bromine water + alkane — still brown.

1) They're made up of _chains_ of carbon atoms with _single_ covalent bonds between them.
2) They're called _saturated_ hydrocarbons because they have _no_ spare bonds left.
3) This is also why they _don't_ decolourise _bromine water_ — _no_ spare bonds.
4) They _won't_ form polymers — same reason again, _no_ spare bonds.
5) The first four alkanes are _methane_ (natural gas), _ethane_, _propane_ and _butane_.
6) They burn cleanly producing _carbon dioxide_ and _water_.

1) Methane
Formula: CH_4

```
    H
    |
H – C – H      (natural
    |            gas)
    H
```

2) Ethane
Formula: C_2H_6

```
    H   H
    |   |
H – C – C – H
    |   |
    H   H
```

3) Propane
Formula: C_3H_8

```
    H   H   H
    |   |   |
H – C – C – C – H
    |   |   |
    H   H   H
```

4) Butane
Formula: C_4H_{10}

```
    H   H   H   H
    |   |   |   |
H – C – C – C – C – H
    |   |   |   |
    H   H   H   H
```

ALKENES have a C=C DOUBLE bond

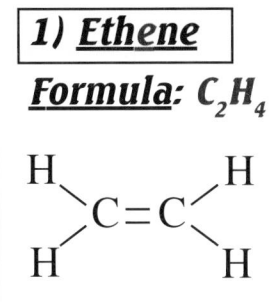

Bromine water + alkene — decolourised

1) They're _chains_ of carbon atoms with some _double_ bonds.
2) They are called _unsaturated_ hydrocarbons because they have some _spare_ bonds left.
3) This is why they will decolourise _bromine water_. They form _bonds_ with bromide ions.
4) They form _polymers_ by _opening up_ their double bonds to "_hold hands_" in a long chain.
5) The first three alkenes are _ethene_, _propene_ and _butene_.
6) They tend to burn with a _smoky flame_, producing _soot_ (carbon).

1) Ethene
Formula: C_2H_4

```
 H             H
  \           /
   C  =  C
  /           \
 H             H
```

2) Propene
Formula: C_3H_6

```
    H   H
    |   |      H
H – C – C = C
    |          \
    H           H
```

3) Butene
Formula: C_4H_8

```
    H   H       H
    |   |       |
H – C – C = C – C – H
    |           |
    H           H   H
```

IMPORTANT POINTS to be noted:

1) _Bromine water_ is the _standard_ test to distinguish between alkanes and alkenes.
2) _ALKENES_ are more _reactive_ due to the _double_ bond all poised and ready to just pop open.
3) Notice the names: "_Meth-_" means "_one_ carbon atom", "_eth-_" means "_two_ C atoms" , "_prop-_" means "_three_ C atoms", "_but-_" means "_four_ C atoms", etc. The only difference then between the names of _alkanes_ and _alkenes_ is just the "-_ane_" or "-_ene_" on the end.
4) _ALL ALKANES_ have the formula: C_nH_{2n+2} _ALL ALKENES_ have the formula: C_nH_{2n}

Alkane anybody who doesn't learn this lot properly...

Six details and three or four structural diagrams for alkanes and alkenes, plus four extra points.
It really isn't that difficult to learn the whole page until you can scribble it down from memory.
Try doing it for five minutes: _Learn, cover, scribble, check, relearn, cover, scribble, check, etc._

Polymers and Plastics

Polymers and plastics were first discovered in about 1933. By 1970 it was all too late. Those halcyon days when they made *proper* motor cars with leather seats and lovely wooden dashboards were over. Sigh.

Alkenes open their double bonds to form Polymers

Under a bit of _pressure_ and with a bit of a _catalyst_ to help it along, many _small alkenes_ will open up their _double bonds_ and "join hands" to form _very long chains_ called _polymers_. There's a couple of important points worth knowing here:

1) The process of joining up lots of _individual alkenes_ to form a _plastic_ is called _polymerisation_.
2) If _no other products_ are formed during the polymerisation reaction, the process is called _addition polymerisation_.
3) The _individual_ units which "hold hands" to form the polymer are called _monomers_.

Ethene becoming polyethene or "polythene" is the easiest example of polymerisation:

Many single ethenes → Pressure and Catalyst → Polyethene

$$n\left(\begin{array}{c}|\\C=C\\|\end{array}\right) \longrightarrow \left(\begin{array}{c}|\\C-C\\|\end{array}\right)_n$$

Many single ethenes   Polyethene

There are loads of Plastics with loads of different uses

1) Polythene: Plastic bags   Bottles   Buckets   Bowls

1) Made from _ethene_
2) Very _cheap_ and _strong_
3) Easily _moulded_

2) PVC: Wellington boots   Raincoats   Electrical equipment

1) A _flexible_ and _shiny_ polymer
2) Again, a _cheap_ plastic
3) Good _electrical insulator_
4) _Dangerous_ if burned

  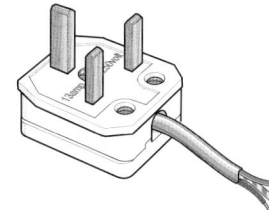

Revision — it's all about stringing lots of facts together...

Learn what polymerisation is and practise the set of diagrams for ethene. Also learn all the examples given for the different types of plastics. _Then cover the page and scribble it all down._

Metal Ores from the Ground

Rocks, Minerals and Ores

1) A _rock_ is a mixture of _minerals_.
2) A _mineral_ is any _solid element or compound_ found naturally in the _Earth's crust_.
   Examples: Diamond (carbon), quartz (silicon dioxide), bauxite (Al_2O_3).
3) A _metal ore_ is defined as a _mineral_ or minerals which contain _enough metal_ in them to make it _worthwhile_ extracting the metal from it.

Metals are extracted using Carbon or Electrolysis

1) _Extracting a metal_ from its ore involves a _chemical reaction_ to separate the metal out.
2) In many cases the metal is found as an _oxide_. There are three ores you need to know:

   a) _Iron ore_ is called _Haematite_, which is iron (III) oxide, formula Fe_2O_3.
   b) _Aluminium ore_ is called _Bauxite_, which is aluminium oxide, formula Al_2O_3.
   c) _Copper ore_ is called _Malachite_, which is copper (II) carbonate, formula $CuCO_3$.

3) The _TWO_ common ways of _extracting a metal_ from its ore are:
   a) Chemical _reduction_ using _carbon_ or _carbon monoxide_ (e.g. iron),
   b) _Electrolysis_ (breaking the ore down by passing an electric current through it).

4) _Gold_ is one of the few metals found as a _metal_ rather than in a chemical compound (an ore).

More Reactive Metals are Harder to Get

1) The _more reactive_ metals took _longer_ to be discovered (e.g. aluminium, sodium).
2) The _more reactive_ metals are also _harder to extract_ from their mineral ores.
3) The above _two facts_ are obviously _related_. It's _obvious_ when you think about it...

Primitive man could find gold easy enough just lying about in streams and then melt it into ingots and jewellery whilst watching Mrs Ug cook his mammoth-tail soup, but realistically building a fully operational electrolysis plant to extract sodium metal from rock salt was unlikely to develop from his daily routine of hunting and cooking.

The Position of Carbon In the Reactivity Series decides it...

1) Metals _higher than carbon_ in the reactivity series have to be extracted using _electrolysis_.

2) Metals _below carbon_ in the reactivity series can be extracted by _reduction_ using _carbon_.

3) This is obviously because carbon _can only take the oxygen_ away from metals which are _less reactive_ than carbon _itself_ is.

The Reactivity Series	
Potassium	K
Sodium	Na
Calcium	Ca
Magnesium	Mg
Aluminium	Al
CARBON	C
Zinc	Zn
Iron	Fe
Tin	Sn
Lead	Pb

Extracted using _Electrolysis_

Extracted by _reduction_ using _carbon_

Higher Higher

Miners — they always have to get their ore in...

This page has four sections with three or four important points in each.
They're all important enough to need learning (except the bit about the soup, etc.).
You need to practise _repeating_ the details _from memory_. That's the _only effective method_.

Iron — The Blast Furnace

Iron is a _very common element_ in the Earth's crust, but good iron ores are only found in _a few select places_ around the world, such as Australia, Canada and Millom.
Iron is extracted from _haematite_, Fe_2O_3, by _reduction_ (i.e. removal of oxygen) in a _blast furnace_.
You really do need to know all these details about what goes on in a blast furnace, _including the equations_.

The Raw Materials are Iron Ore, Coke and Limestone

1) The iron ore contains the _iron_ which is pretty important.
2) The _coke_ is almost pure _carbon_. This is for _reducing_ the _iron oxide_ to _iron metal_.
3) The _limestone_ takes away impurities in the form of _slag_.

Reducing the Iron Ore to Iron:

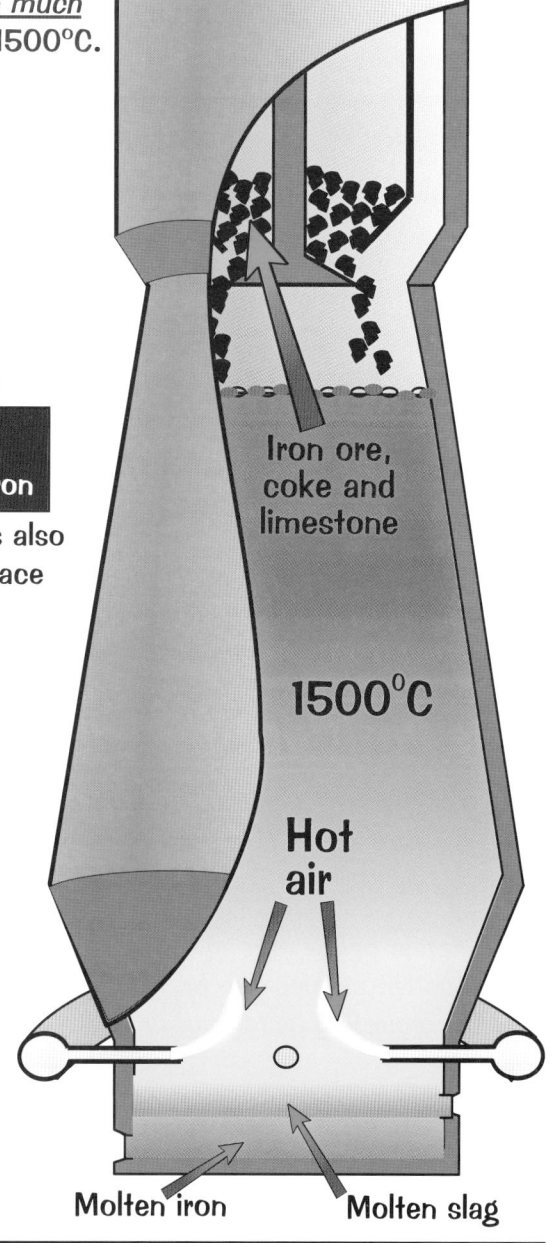

Iron ore, coke and limestone

1500°C

Hot air

Molten iron   Molten slag

1) _Hot air_ is blasted into the furnace making the coke _burn much faster_ than normal and the _temperature rises_ to about 1500°C.

2) The _coke burns_ and produces _carbon dioxide_:

$$C + O_2 \rightarrow CO_2$$
carbon + oxygen → carbon dioxide

3) The CO_2 then reacts with _unburnt coke_ to form _CO_:

$$CO_2 + C \rightarrow 2CO$$
carbon dioxide + carbon → carbon monoxide

4) The _carbon monoxide_ then _reduces_ the _iron ore_ to _iron_:

$$3CO + Fe_2O_3 \rightarrow 3CO_2 + 2Fe$$
carbon monoxide + iron(III)oxide → carbon dioxide + iron

5) The _iron_ is of course _molten_ at this temperature and it's also very _dense_ so it runs straight to the _bottom_ of the furnace where it's _tapped off_.

Removing the Impurities:

1) The _main impurity_ is _sand_, (silicon dioxide). This is still _solid_ even at 1500°C and would tend to stay mixed in with the iron. The limestone removes it.

2) The limestone is _decomposed_ by the _heat_ into _calcium oxide_ and CO_2.

$$CaCO_3 \rightarrow CaO + CO_2$$

3) The _calcium oxide_ then reacts with the _sand_ to form _calcium silicate_ or _slag_ which is molten and can be tapped off:

$$CaO + SiO_2 \rightarrow CaSiO_3 \text{ (molten slag)}$$

4) The cooled slag is _solid_, and is used for:
   1) _Road building_   2) _Fertiliser_

Learn the facts about Iron Extraction — it's a blast...

Three main sections and several numbered points for each. Every bit of it is important and could be tested in the Exam, including the equations. Use the _mini-essay_ method for each section. Alternatively, cover it up one section at a time, and try _repeating the facts_ back to yourself. _And keep trying_.

Extracting Aluminium

A Molten State is needed for Electrolysis

1) _Aluminium_ is more _reactive_ than _carbon_ so it has to be extracted from its ore by _electrolysis_.
2) The basic ore is _bauxite_, and after mining and purifying a white powder is left.
3) This is pure aluminium oxide, Al_2O_3, which has a _very high_ melting point of over 2000°C.
4) For _electrolysis_ to work a _molten state_ is required, and heating to 2000°C would be _expensive_.

Cryolite is used to lower the temperature (and costs)

1) Instead, the aluminium oxide is _dissolved_ in _molten cryolite_ (a less common ore of aluminium).
2) This brings the temperature _down_ to about 900°C, which makes it _much_ cheaper and easier.
3) The _electrodes_ are made of _graphite_ (carbon).
4) The graphite _anode_ (+ve) does need _replacing_ quite often. It keeps _reacting_ to form CO_2.

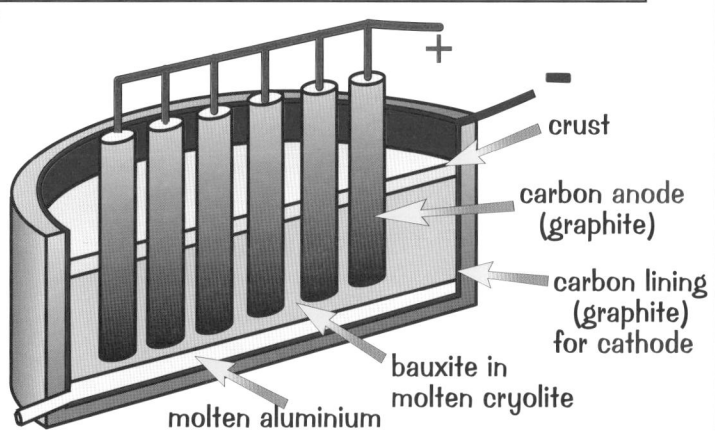

crust

carbon anode (graphite)

carbon lining (graphite) for cathode

bauxite in molten cryolite

molten aluminium

Electrolysis — turning IONS into the ATOMS you want

This is the _main object_ of the exercise:

1) Make the aluminium oxide _molten_ to _release_ the aluminium _ions_, Al^{3+} so they're _free_ to move.

2) Stick _electrodes_ in — so that the _positive_ Al^{3+} _ions_ will head straight for the _negative electrode_.

3) At the negative electrode they just can't help picking up some of the _spare electrons_ and 'zup', they've turned into aluminium _atoms_ and they _sink to the bottom_. Pretty clever, I think.

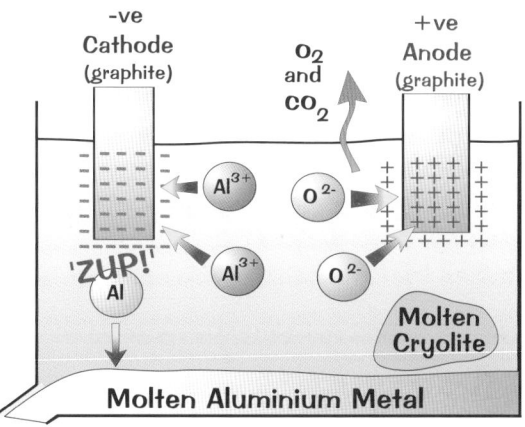

-ve Cathode (graphite)

O_2 and CO_2

+ve Anode (graphite)

Al^{3+}

O^{2-}

'ZUP!' Al

Al^{3+}

O^{2-}

Molten Cryolite

Molten Aluminium Metal

Overall, this is a _REDOX reaction_ and you need to know the _reactions_ at both electrodes:

Higher

At the Cathode (–ve):

$$Al^{3+} + 3e^- \rightarrow Al$$

(_REDUCTION_ — a gain of electrons)

At the Anode (+ve):

$$2O^{2-} \rightarrow O_2 + 4e^-$$

(_OXIDATION_ — a loss of electrons)

Higher

Electrolysis aint cheap — well, there's always a charge...

Four main sections with several important points to learn for each. Initially you might find it easiest to cover the sections one at a time and try to _recall the details_ in your head. Ultimately though you should _aim to repeat it all in one go_ with the whole page covered.

Purifying Copper by Electrolysis

1) Aluminium is a _very reactive metal_ and _has_ to be removed from its ore by _electrolysis_.
2) _Copper_ is a very _unreactive_ metal. Not only is it below carbon in the reactivity series, it's also below _hydrogen_, which means that copper doesn't even react with _water_.
3) So copper is obtained _very easily_ from its ore by _reduction_ with _carbon_.

Very pure copper is needed for electrical conductors

1) The copper produced by _reduction isn't pure enough_ for use in _electrical conductors_.
2) The _purer_ it is, the better it _conducts_. _Electrolysis_ is used to obtain _very pure copper_.

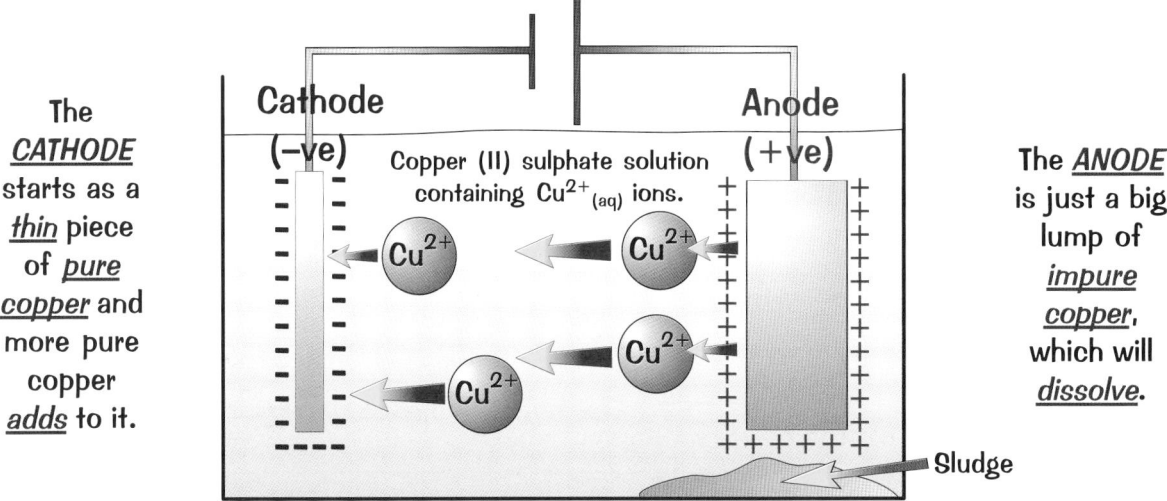

The _CATHODE_ starts as a _thin_ piece of _pure copper_ and more pure copper _adds_ to it.

The _ANODE_ is just a big lump of _impure copper_, which will _dissolve_.

Sludge

The _ELECTRICAL SUPPLY_ acts by:

1) _Pulling electrons off_ copper atoms at the _anode_ causing them to go into solution as _Cu²⁺ ions_.
2) Then _offering electrons_ at the _cathode_ to nearby _Cu²⁺ ions_ to turn them back into _copper atoms_.
3) The _impurities_ are dropped at the _anode_ as a _sludge_, whilst _pure copper atoms_ bond to the _cathode_.
4) The electrolysis can go on for _weeks_ and the cathode is often _twenty times bigger_ at the end of it.

Pure copper is deposited on the pure cathode (–ve)

Copper dissolves from the impure anode (+ve)

The reaction at the _CATHODE_ is:

$$Cu^{2+}_{(aq)} + 2e^- \rightarrow Cu_{(s)}$$

This is an example of _REDuction_. The copper ions have been _reduced_ to copper atoms by _gaining_ electrons.

The reaction at the _ANODE_ is:

$$Cu_{(s)} \rightarrow Cu^{2+}_{(aq)} + 2e^-$$

Copper atoms have been _OXidised_ into copper atoms by _gaining_ electrons. Overall, this is an example of a _REDOX_ reaction (more on this later).

Revision and Electrolysis — they can both go on for weeks...

This is a pretty easy page to learn. The mini-essay method will do you proud here. Don't forget the diagram and the equations. I know it's not much fun, but think how useful all this chemistry will be in your day-to-day life once you've learned it...
... hmmm, well... _learn it anyway_.

Uses of The Three Common Metals

Metals are a lot more interesting than most people ever realise.   (Classic chat-up line No. 71)

Iron is made into steel which is cheap and strong

IRON AND STEEL:
     ADVANTAGES: _Cheap_ and _strong_.
     DISADVANTAGES: _Heavy_, and prone to _rusting away_.

Iron and steel are used for:
1) _Construction_ such as bridges and buildings.
2) _Cars_ and _lorries_ and _trains_ and _boats_ and NOT PLANES and _pushbikes_ and _tanks_ and _pianos_...
3) _Stainless steel_ doesn't rust and is used for pans and for fixtures on boats.

Steel may rust and it may not be exactly "space age" but it's strong and it's awful cheap, and it still has a lot of uses. They make cars out of it for one thing... but gone are the halcyon days when car bodies were hand-crafted from ash frames and lovingly honed to perfection. Now they just shovel them out of big presses by the million. Sigh.   Mind you there's still the Morgan...

Aluminium is light, strong and corrosion-resistant

Strictly speaking you shouldn't say it's 'light', you should say it has '_low density_'.
Whatever. All I know is, it's a _lot_ easier to lift and move around than iron or steel.

USEFUL PROPERTIES:
1) Lightweight.   (OK, '_low density_'. Happy now?)
2) Can be _bent_ and _shaped_ (for making car body panels, etc.)
3) _Strong_ and very rigid when required.
4) _DOESN'T CORRODE_ due to the protective layer of _oxide_ which always quickly covers it.
5) It's also a _good conductor_ of heat and electricity.

DRAWBACKS: _Not as strong_ as steel and a bit more _expensive_.
COMMON USES:
1) _Ladders_.
2) _Aeroplanes_.
3) Range Rover _body panels_ (but not the rusty tailgate!).
4) _Drink cans_ — better than tin-plated steel ones which can rust if damaged.
5) _Greenhouses_ and _window frames_.
6) Big _power cables_ used on pylons.

Copper: good conductor, easily bent and doesn't corrode

This is a winning combination which makes it ideal for:

1) _Water pipes_ and _gas pipes_, because it can be _bent to shape_ by hand without fracturing.
2) _Electrical wiring_ because it can be easily _bent_ round corners and it _conducts_ really well.
3) Forms useful _non corroding_ alloys such as _brass_ (for trumpets) and _bronze_ (for statues).

DRAWBACKS: Copper is quite _expensive_ and is _not strong_.

The Exciting Properties of Metals — learn and enjoy...

Well now, what have we here! Some chemistry which _IS_ useful in your everyday life!   I reckon it's really pretty helpful if you know the difference between various different metals, although I guess it's only really important if you plan to build your own steam engine or rocket or something.
If you don't, then you'll just have to _learn it for the Exam_ and be done with it.

The Haber Process

This is an *important industrial process*. It produces *ammonia* which is needed for making *fertilisers*.

Nitrogen and Hydrogen are needed to make Ammonia

1) The *nitrogen* is obtained easily from the *AIR*, which is *78% nitrogen* (and 21% oxygen).
2) The *hydrogen* is obtained from *WATER* (steam) and *NATURAL GAS* (methane, CH_4).
   The methane and steam are reacted *together* like this:

$$CH_{4\,(g)} + H_2O_{(g)} \rightarrow CO_{(g)} + 3H_{2\,(g)}$$

3) Hydrogen can also be obtained from *crude oil*.

The Haber Process is a Reversible Reaction:

$$N_{2\,(g)} + 3H_{2\,(g)} \rightleftharpoons 2NH_{3\,(g)} \quad (+ \text{ heat})$$

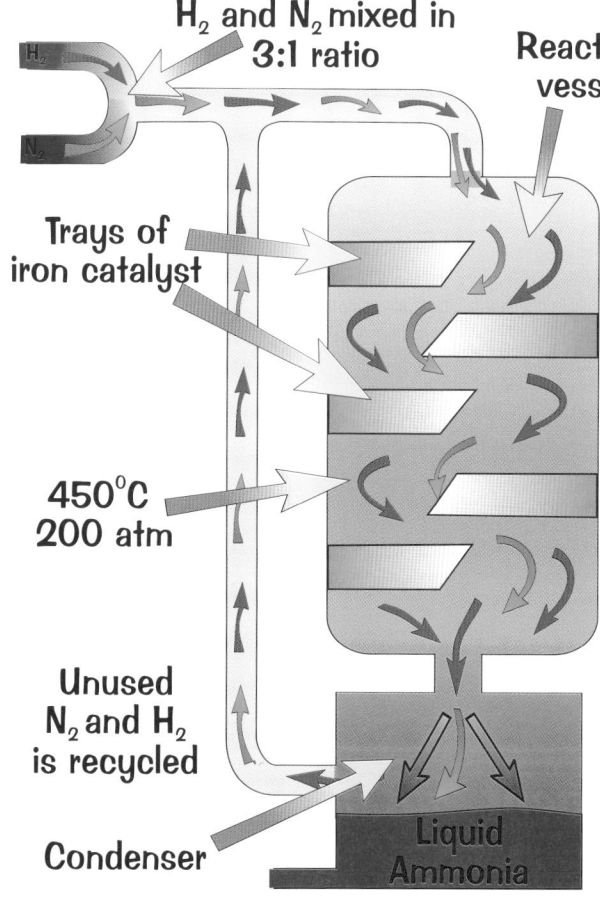

H$_2$ and N$_2$ mixed in 3:1 ratio

Reaction vessel

Trays of iron catalyst

450°C 200 atm

Unused N$_2$ and H$_2$ is recycled

Condenser

Liquid Ammonia

Higher Higher

Higher Higher

Industrial conditions:

PRESSURE:	200 atmospheres
TEMPERATURE:	450°C
CATALYST:	Iron

Because the Reaction is Reversible, there's a compromise to be made:

1) *Higher pressures* favour the *forward* reaction, hence the *200 atmospheres* operating pressure.

2) However, it turns out that *lower* temperatures improve the forward reaction. At least it does in terms of the *proportion* of hydrogen and nitrogen converting to ammonia. This is called the *yield*.

3) The trouble is, *lower temperatures* mean a *slower rate of reaction*. (This is different from *yield*.)

4) So the 450°C is a *compromise* between *maximum yield* and *speed of reaction*.

5) The pressure used is also a compromise. Even *higher* pressures would *increase* the yield further, but the plant would be *more expensive to build*. In the end it all comes down to *minimising costs*.

There's more on the *economics of the Haber Process* on P. 85 - 86.

EXTRA NOTES:

1) The hydrogen and nitrogen are mixed together in a *3:1 ratio*.
2) Because the reaction is *reversible*, not all of the nitrogen and hydrogen will *convert* to ammonia.
3) The *ammonia* is formed as a *gas* but as it cools in the condenser it *liquefies* and is *removed*.
4) The N$_2$ and H$_2$ which didn't react are *recycled* and passed through again so *none is wasted*.

200 atmospheres? — that could give you a headache..

There are quite a lot of details on this page. They're pretty keen on the Haber process in the Exams so you'd be well advised to learn all this. They could easily ask you on any of these details. Use the same good old method: *Learn it, cover it up, repeat it back to yourself, check, try again...*

Fertiliser from Ammonia

On this page are *two reactions* involving *ammonia* that you need to be familiar with. Somehow, I don't think I'd have either of them in my list of "Top Ten Most Riveting Chemistry Topics":

1) Ammonia Can be Oxidised To Form Nitric Acid

There are *two stages* to this reaction:

a) Ammonia gas reacts with oxygen over a hot platinum catalyst:

$$4NH_{3 (g)} + 5O_{2 (g)} \rightarrow 4NO_{(g)} + 6H_2O_{(g)}$$

This first stage is very *exothermic* and produces it's own heat to *keep it going*.
The nitrogen monoxide must be *cooled* before the next stage, which happens easily:

b) The nitrogen monoxide reacts with water and oxygen...

$$6NO_{(g)} + 3O_{2 (g)} + 2H_2O_{(g)} \rightarrow 4HNO_{3 (g)} + 2NO_{(g)}$$

...to form nitric acid, HNO_3

Gripping stuff. Anyway, the *nitric acid* produced is *very useful* for other chemical processes. One such use is to make *ammonium nitrate* fertiliser...

2) Ammonia can be neutralised with Nitric Acid...

...to make Ammonium Nitrate fertiliser

This is a straightforward and spectacularly unexciting *neutralisation* reaction between an *alkali* (ammonia) and an *acid*. The result is of course a *neutral salt*:   *(prod me if I fall asleep)*

$$NH_{3 (g)} + HNO_{3 (aq)} \rightarrow NH_4NO_{3 (aq)}$$
Ammonia + Nitric acid → Ammonium nitrate

Ammonium nitrate is an especially good fertiliser because it has *nitrogen* from *two sources*, the ammonia and the nitric acid. Kind of a *double dose*. Plants need nitrogen to make *proteins*.

Excessive Nitrate Fertiliser causes Eutrophication and Health Problems

1) If *nitrate fertilisers* wash into *streams* they set off a cycle of *mega-growth*, *mega-death* and *mega-decay*. Plants and green algae grow out of control, then start to *die off* because there's too many of them, then *bacteria* take over, feeding off the dying plants and using up all the *oxygen* in the water. Then the fish all die because they can't get enough *oxygen*. Lovely. It's called *eutrophication* (see the Biology Book for more details). It's all good clean fun.

2) If too many *nitrates* get into drinking water it can cause *health problems*, especially for young *babies*. Nitrates prevent the *blood* from carrying *oxygen* properly and children can *turn blue* and even *die*.

3) To avoid these problems it's important that artificial nitrate fertilisers are applied *carefully* by all farmers — they must take care not to apply *too much*, and not if it's *going to rain* soon.

There's nowt wrong wi' just spreadin' muck on it...

Basically, this page is about how ammonia is turned into ammonium nitrate fertiliser. Alas there are some seriously tedious details which they seem to expect you to learn. Don't ask me why. Anyway, *the more you learn, the more you know*. (He said, wisely and meaninglessly.)

28

Four Uses Of Limestone

Limestone is a <u>sedimentary rock</u>, formed mainly from <u>sea shells</u>. It is mostly *calcium carbonate*.

1) Limestone Used as a Building Material

1) It's great for making into <u>blocks</u> for building with. Fine old buildings like cathedrals are often made purely from limestone blocks. <u>Acid rain</u> can be a problem though.
2) For <u>statues</u> and fancy carved bits on nice buildings. But <u>acid rain</u> is even *more* of a problem.
3) It can just be crushed up into chippings and used for <u>road surfacing</u>.

2) Limestone for Neutralising Acid in lakes and soil

1) Ordinary limestone ground into <u>powder</u> can be used to <u>neutralise acidity</u> in lakes caused by <u>acid rain</u>. It can also be used to neutralise <u>acid soils</u> in fields.
2) It works <u>better</u> and <u>faster</u> if it's turned into <u>slaked lime</u> first:

Turning Limestone into Slaked Lime: first heat it up, then add water

1) The *limestone*, which is mostly *calcium carbonate*, is *heated* and it turns into *calcium oxide* (CaO):

limestone $\xrightarrow{\text{HEAT}}$ quicklime   or $CaCO_3 \xrightarrow{\text{HEAT}} CaO + CO_2$

2) *Calcium oxide* reacts *violently* with *water* to produce *calcium hydroxide* (or slaked lime):

quicklime + water $\longrightarrow$ slaked lime   or $CaO + H_2O \longrightarrow Ca(OH)_2$

3) <u>Slaked lime</u> is a <u>white powder</u> and can be applied to fields just like powdered limestone.
4) The <u>advantage</u> is that slaked lime acts much <u>faster</u> at reducing the acidity.

3) Limestone and Clay are Heated to Make Cement

1) <u>Clay</u> contains <u>aluminium</u> and <u>silicates</u> and is dug out of the ground.
2) Powdered <u>clay</u> and powdered <u>limestone</u> are <u>roasted</u> in a rotating <u>kiln</u> to produce a complex mixture of calcium and aluminium silicates, called <u>cement</u>.
3) When <u>cement</u> is mixed with <u>water</u> a slow chemical reaction takes place.
4) This causes the cement to gradually <u>set hard</u>.
5) Cement is usually mixed with <u>sand and chippings</u> to make <u>concrete</u>.
6) <u>Concrete</u> is a very quick and cheap way of constructing buildings — and it shows... — concrete has got to be the most hideously unattractive building material ever known.

4) Glass is made by melting Limestone, Sand and Soda

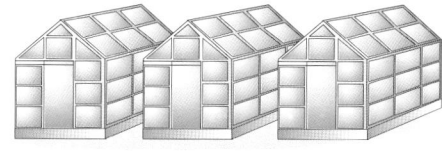

1) Just heat up <u>limestone</u> (calcium carbonate) with <u>sand</u> (silicon dioxide) and <u>soda</u> (sodium carbonate) until it <u>melts</u>.
2) When the mixture cools it comes out as <u>glass</u>. It's as easy as that. Eat your heart out Mr. Pilkington.

Tough Revision here — this stuff's rock hard...

I bet when those little sea creatures died all those millions of years ago, they had no idea they would one day become the cornerstones of 20th century civilisation. Get it! — *cornerstones*. Chortle chortle. Anyway, enough frivolity. <u>Learn the whole page</u> till you've got it *rock solid*...

Revision Summary for Section Two

Section Two is pretty interesting stuff I reckon. Relatively speaking. Anyway, whether it is or it isn't, the only thing that really matters is whether you've learnt it all or not. These questions aren't exactly friendly, but they're a seriously serious way of finding out what you don't know. And don't forget, that's what revision is all about — finding out what you don't know and then learning it till you do. Practise these questions as often as necessary — not just once. Your ultimate aim is to be able to answer all of them easily.

1) What are fossil fuels? Why are they called fossil fuels?
2) Describe how fossil fuels were formed. What length of time did it take?
3) Give details of how all three types of fossil fuels are extracted.
4) What does crude oil consist of?
5) Draw the full diagram of fractional distillation of crude oil.
6) What are the seven main fractions obtained from crude oil, and what are they used for?
7) What are hydrocarbons? Describe four properties and how they vary with the molecule size.
8) Give the equations for complete and incomplete combustion of hydrocarbons.
9) Which type is dangerous and why? What are the flames for these two types of combustion?
10) What is "cracking"? Why is it done?
11) Give a typical example of a substance which is cracked and the products that you get.
12) What are the industrial conditions used for cracking?
13) What are alkanes and alkenes? What is the basic difference between them?
14) Draw the structures of the first four alkanes and the first three alkenes and give their names.
15) List four differences in the chemical properties of alkanes an alkenes.
16) What are polymers? What kind of substances can form polymers?
17) Draw diagrams to show how ethene and propene form polymers.
18) Name two types of plastic, give their physical properties and say what they're used for.
19) What are rocks, ores and minerals? Which metal is found as a metal rather than an ore?
20) What are the two methods for extracting metals from their ores?
21) What property of the metal decides which method is needed?
22) Draw a diagram of a blast furnace. What are the three raw materials used in it?
23) Write down the equations for how iron is obtained from its ore in the blast furnace.
24) What is slag? Write two equations for the formation of slag, and give two uses of it.
25) How is aluminium extracted from its ore? Give four operational details and draw a diagram.
26) Explain how aluminium metal is obtained from the process, and give the two equations.
27) Explain three reasons why this process is so expensive.
28) How is copper extracted from its ore? How is it then purified, and why does it need to be?
29) Draw a diagram for the purifying process.
30) Give the two equations relevant to the electrolysis of copper.
31) Describe how the pure copper is obtained.
32) Describe the plus and minus points of iron (and steel), and give six uses for it.
33) Describe the plus and minus points of aluminium, and give six uses for it.
34) Describe the plus and minus points of copper, and give three uses for it.
35) What is the Haber process? What are the raw materials for it and how are they obtained?
36) Draw a full diagram for the Haber process and explain the temperature and pressure used.
37) Give full details of how ammonia is turned into nitric acid, including equations.
38) What is the main use of ammonia? Give the equation for producing ammonium nitrate.
39) Give two problems resulting from the use of nitrate fertilisers.
40) What are the four main uses of limestone?
41) Give the equations for turning limestone into slaked lime. Why do we bother?
42) Give four details about what cement is made of and how it works.

Nine Types of Chemical Change

There are *nine* types of chemical change you should know about. It's well worth learning exactly what each of them is, *here and now*, rather than living the rest of your life in a confused haze.

1) *THERMAL DECOMPOSITION* — *breakdown on heating*

This is when a substance *breaks down* into simpler substances *when heated*, often with the help of a *catalyst*. It's different from a reaction because there's only *one substance* to start with. Cracking of hydrocarbons is a good example of thermal decomposition.

2) *NEUTRALISATION* — *acid + alkali gives salt +water*

This is simply when an *acid* reacts with an *alkali* (or base) to form a *neutral* product, which is neither acid nor alkali (usually a *salt* solution). More on this later.

3) *DISPLACEMENT* — *one metal kicking another one out*

This is a reaction where a *more reactive* element reacts with a compound and *pushes out* a *less reactive* "rival" element. *Metals* are the most common example. Magnesium will react with iron sulphate to push the iron out and form magnesium sulphate.

4) *PRECIPITATION* — *solid forms in solution*

This is a reaction where two *solutions* react and a *solid* forms in the solution and *sinks*. The solid is said to *"PRECIPITATE OUT"* and, confusingly, the solid is also called *"a precipitate"*.

5) *OXIDATION* — *loss of electrons*

Oxidation is the *addition of oxygen*. Iron becoming iron oxide is oxidation. The more technical and general definition of oxidation is '*the LOSS of electrons*'.

6) *REDUCTION* — *gain of electrons*

Reduction is the *reverse of oxidation*, i.e. the *loss of oxygen*. Iron oxide is *reduced* to iron. The more technical and general definition of reduction is '*the GAIN of electrons*'. Note that reduction is *gain* of electrons. That's the way to remember it — it's kinda the wrong way round.

7) *EXOTHERMIC REACTIONS* — *give out heat*

Exothermic reactions give *out energy*, usually as heat. "Exo-" as in "Exit", or "out". Any time a *fuel burns* and *gives off heat* it's an *exothermic* reaction.

8) *ENDOTHERMIC REACTIONS* — *take in heat*

Endothermic reactions need heat putting *in* constantly to make them work. Heat is needed to *form* chemical bonds. The *products* of endothermic reactions are likely to be *more useful* than the *reactants*, otherwise we wouldn't bother putting all the energy in, e.g. turning *iron oxide* into *iron* is an endothermic process. We need a lot of heat from the coke to keep it happening.

9) *REVERSIBLE REACTIONS* — *they go both ways*

Reversible reactions are ones that will cheerfully go in *both* directions at the *same time*. In other words, the *products* can easily turn back into the *original reactants*.

Nine more fantastic chat-up lines just waiting to happen...

A nice easy page to learn. You should know a lot of this already.
Anyway, cover the page and expose each yellow box (*without* the other bit of the heading!) one by one and try to explain it to yourself before uncovering the text to check.

Chemical Equations

Equations need a lot of *practice* if you're going to get them right. They can get *real tricky* real quickly, unless you *really* know your stuff. Every time you do an equation you need to *practice* getting it *right* rather than skating over it.

Chemical formulae tell you how many atoms there are

1) Hydrogen chloride has the chemical formula HCl. This means that in any molecule of hydrogen chloride there will be: <u>one</u> atom of hydrogen bonded to <u>one</u> atom of chlorine.

2) Ammonia has the formula NH_3. This means that in any molecule of ammonia there will be: *three* atoms of hydrogen bonded to *one* atom of nitrogen. Simple.

3) A chemical reaction can be described by the process *reactants* → *products*.

     e.g.   methane *reacts* with oxygen to *produce* carbon dioxide and water

     e.g.   magnesium *reacts* with oxygen to *produce* magnesuim oxide.

You have to know how to write these reactions in both words and symbols, as shown below:

The Symbol Equation shows the atoms on both sides:

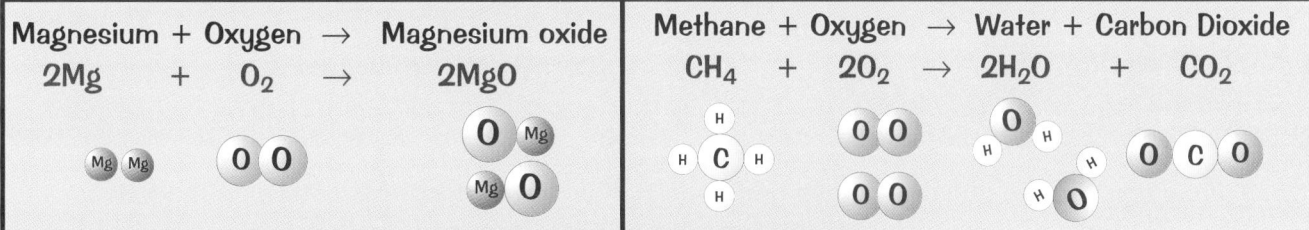

Magnesium + Oxygen → Magnesium oxide
$$2Mg + O_2 \rightarrow 2MgO$$

Methane + Oxygen → Water + Carbon Dioxide
$$CH_4 + 2O_2 \rightarrow 2H_2O + CO_2$$

You need to know how to write out any Equation...

You *really* do need to know how to write out chemical equations. In fact you need to know how to write out equations for pretty well all the reactions in this book.

That might sound like an awful lot, but there aren't nearly as many as you think. Have a look.

You also need to know the *formulae* for all the *ionic* and *covalent* compounds in here too. Lovely.

State Symbols tell you what Physical State it's in

These are easy enough, *just make sure you know them*, especially aq (aqueous).

(s) — Solid	(l) — Liquid	(g) — Gas	(aq) — Dissloved in water

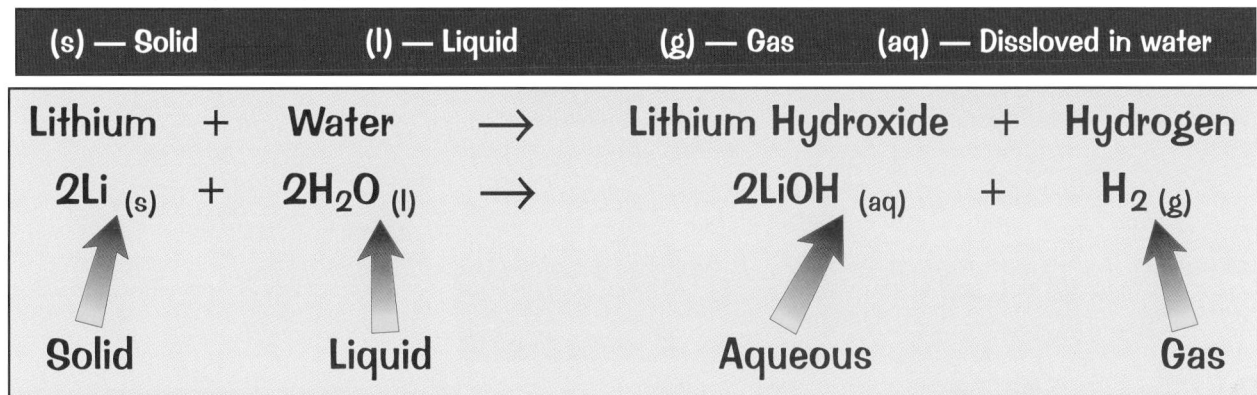

Lithium + Water → Lithium Hydroxide + Hydrogen
$$2Li_{(s)} + 2H_2O_{(l)} \rightarrow 2LiOH_{(aq)} + H_{2(g)}$$

Solid   Liquid   Aqueous   Gas

It's tricky — but don't get yourself in a state over it...

Make sure you know the formulae for *all* the ionic and covalent compounds you've come across so far. And for *higher* level, write symbol equations for the following equations and put the state symbols in too: 1) Iron(III) oxide + hydrogen → iron + water

2) Dilute hydrochloric acid + aluminium → aluminium chloride + hydrogen (answers on P.90)

Balancing Equations

Things start to get a wee bit tricky now. Hang in there and remember... *practice makes perfect*.

Balancing The Equation — match them up one by one

1) There must always be the *same* number of atoms on *both sides*, they can't just *disappear*.
2) You *balance* the equation by putting numbers **IN FRONT** of the formulae where needed.
   Take this equation for reacting sulphuric acid with sodium hydroxide:

$$H_2SO_4 + NaOH \rightarrow Na_2SO_4 + H_2O$$

The *formulae* are all correct but the numbers of some atoms *don't match up* on both sides.
You *can't change formulae* like H_2SO_4 to H_2SO_5. You can only put numbers *in front of them*:

Method: Balance just ONE type of atom at a time

The more you practise, the quicker you get, but all you do is this:

1) Find an element that *doesn't balance* and *pencil in a number* to try and sort it out.
2) *See where it gets you*. It may create *another imbalance* but pencil in *another number* and see where that gets you.
3) Carry on chasing *unbalanced* elements and it'll *sort itself out* pretty quickly.

I'll show you. In the equation above you soon notice we're short of H atoms on the RHS.
1) The only thing you can do about that is make it $2H_2O$ instead of just H_2O:

$$H_2SO_4 + NaOH \rightarrow Na_2SO_4 + 2H_2O$$

2) But that now causes too many H atoms and O atoms on the RHS, so to balance that up you could try putting $2NaOH$ on the LHS (Left Hand Side):

$$H_2SO_4 + 2NaOH \rightarrow Na_2SO_4 + 2H_2O$$

3) And suddenly there it is! *Everything balances*. And you'll notice the Na just sorted itself out.

Electrolysis Equations — make sure the electrons balance

The main thing is to make sure the *number of electrons* is the *same* for *both half-equations*.
For the cell shown the basic half equations are:

CATHODE: $\quad H^+_{(aq)} + e^- \rightarrow H$
ANODE: $\quad\quad\quad\quad Cl^-_{(aq)} \rightarrow Cl + e^-$

These equations *aren't finished* because both the hydrogen and the chlorine come off as *gases*. They must be *rewritten* with H_2 and Cl_2, like this:

CATHODE: $\quad 2H^+ + 2e^- \rightarrow H_{2\,(g)}$
ANODE: $\quad\quad\quad 2Cl^-_{(aq)} \rightarrow Cl_{2\,(g)} + 2e^-$

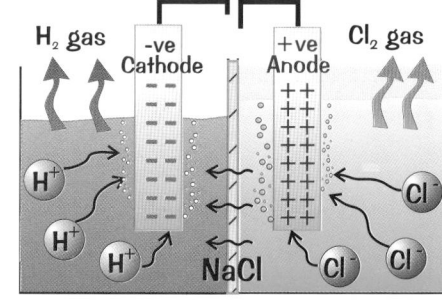

Note that there are *two electrons* in *both* half equations, which means they're nice and *balanced*. This gives the *OVERALL EQUATION*:

$$2HCl_{(aq)} \rightarrow H_{2\,(g)} + Cl_{2\,(g)}$$

Cations — sounds like a useful form of pet control...

Practise scribbling down all these details, *mini-essay* style. Electrolysis can be a bit confusing.
I think you have to make an effort to learn all the details, especially how the two half equations are really just *one* equation, but it kind of happens in two places, *joined by a battery*.

Relative Formula Mass

The biggest trouble with _RELATIVE ATOMIC MASS_ and _RELATIVE FORMULA MASS_ is that they _sound_ so bloodcurdling. _"With big scary names like that they must be really, really complicated"_ I hear you cry. Nope, wrong. They're dead easy. Take a few deep breaths, and just enjoy, as the mists slowly clear...

Relative Atomic Mass, A_r — _easy peasy_

1) This is just a way of saying how _heavy_ different atoms are _compared to each other_.
2) The _relative atomic mass_ A_r is nothing more than the _mass number_ of the element.
3) On the periodic table, the elements all have _two_ numbers. The smaller one is the atomic number (how many protons it has).
   But the _bigger one_ is the _mass number_ (how many protons and neutrons it has) which, kind of obviously, is also the _Relative atomic mass_. Easy peasy, I'd say.

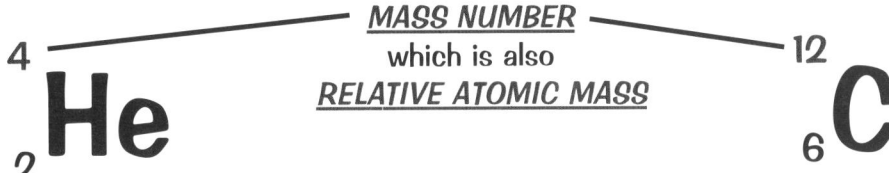

Helium has $A_r = 4$. Carbon has $A_r = 12$. (So carbon atoms are _3 times heavier_ than helium atoms)

Relative Formula Mass, M_r — _also easy peasy_

If you have a compound like $MgCl_2$ then it has a _RELATIVE FORMULA MASS_, M_r, which is just all the relative atomic masses _added together_.
For $MgCl_2$ it would be:

MgCl$_2$

$24 + (35.5 \times 2) = 95$

So the M_r for $MgCl_2$ is simply <u>95</u>

You can easily get the A_r for any element from the _Periodic Table_ (see inside front cover), but in a lot of questions they give you them anyway. I tell you what, since it's nearly Christmas I'll run through another example for you:

Question: _Find the relative formula mass for calcium carbonate, CaCO₃ using the given data:_
A_r for Ca = 40 A_r for C = 12 A_r for O = 16

<u>ANSWER:</u>

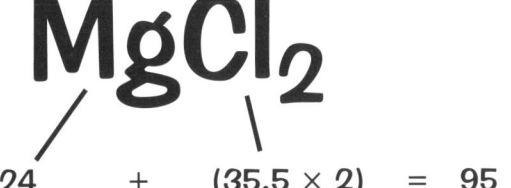

$40 + 12 + (16 \times 3) = 100$

So the Relative Formula Mass for CaCO₃ is <u>100</u>

And that's all it is. A big fancy name like _Relative Formula Mass_ and all it means is _"add up all the mass numbers"_. What a swizz, eh? You'd have thought it'd be something a bit juicier than that, wouldn't you. Still, that's life — it's all a big disappointment in the end. Sigh.

Phew, Chemistry — scary stuff sometimes, innit...

When you know it, _cover the page_ and _scribble down_ the important details. D'ya miss any?
1) Use the periodic table to find the relative atomic mass of these elements: Cu, K, Kr, Fe, Cl
2) Also find the relative formula mass of these compounds: NaOH, Fe_2O_3, C_6H_{14}, $Mg(NO_3)_2$

Two Formula Mass Calculations

Although Relative Atomic Mass and Relative Formula Mass are *easy enough*, it can get just a tadge *trickier* when you start getting into other calculations which use them. It depends on how good your maths is basically, because it's all to do with ratios and percentages.

Calculating % Mass of an Element in a Compound

This is actually dead easy — so long as you've learnt this formula:

$$\text{PERCENTAGE MASS OF AN ELEMENT IN A COMPOUND} = \frac{A_r \times \text{No. of atoms (of that element)}}{M_r \text{ (of whole compound)}} \times 100$$

If you don't learn the formula then you'd better be pretty smart — or you'll struggle.

EXAMPLE: *Find the percentage mass of sodium in sodium carbonate, Na_2CO_3*
ANSWER:
  A_r of sodium = 23, A_r of carbon = 12, A_r of oxygen = 16
  M_r of Na_2CO_3 = $(2\times23)+12+(3\times16)=106$

Now use the formula: $\text{Percentage mass} = \frac{A_r \times n}{M_r}\times100 = \frac{23\times2}{106}\times100 = 43.4\%$

And there you have it. Sodium represents *43.4%* of the mass of sodium carbonate.

Finding The Empirical Formula (from Masses or Percentages)

This also sounds a lot worse than it really is. Try this for an easy peasy *stepwise method*:

1) *LIST ALL THE ELEMENTS* in the compound (there's usually only two or three!)
2) *Underneath them*, write their *EXPERIMENTAL MASSES OR PERCENTAGES*.
3) *DIVIDE* each mass or percentage *BY THE A_r* for that particular element.
4) Turn the numbers you get into *A NICE SIMPLE RATIO* by multiplying and/or dividing them by well-chosen numbers.
5) Get the ratio in its *SIMPLEST FORM*, and that tells you the formula of the compound.

EXAMPLE: *Find the empirical formula of the iron oxide produced when 44.8g of iron react with 19.2g of oxygen. (A_r for iron = 56, A_r for oxygen =16)*
METHOD:

	Fe	O
1) List the two elements:	Fe	O
2) Write in the *experimental masses*:	44.8	19.2
3) Divide by the A_r for each element:	$44.8/56=0.8$	$19.2/16=1.2$
4) Multiply by 10...	8	12
...then divide by 4:	2	3

5) So the *simplest formula* is 2 atoms of Fe to 3 atoms of O, i.e. Fe_2O_3. And that's it done.

> You need to realise (for the Exam) that this *EMPIRICAL METHOD* (i.e. based on *experiment*) is the *only way* of finding out the formula of a compound. Rust is iron oxide, sure, but is it FeO, or Fe_2O_3? Only an experiment to determine the empirical formula will tell you for certain.

Old Dmitri Mendeleev did this sort of stuff in his sleep — the old rogue...

Make sure you *learn the formula* at the top and the five rules in the red box. Then try these:
1) Find the percentage mass of oxygen in these: a) Fe_2O_3 b) H_2O c) $CaCO_3$ d) H_2SO_4
2) Find the empirical formula when 2.4g of carbon reacts with 0.8g of hydrogen.

Calculating Masses in Reactions

These can be kinda scary too, but chill out, little white-faced one — just relax and enjoy.

The Three Important Steps — not to be missed...

(Miss one out and it'll all go horribly wrong, believe me)

> 1) *WRITE OUT* the balanced *EQUATION*
> 2) *Work out M$_r$* — just for the *TWO BITS YOU WANT*
> 3) Apply the rule: *DIVIDE TO GET ONE, THEN MULTIPLY TO GET ALL*
>
> (But you have to apply this first to the substance they give information about, and *then* the other one!)

EXAMPLE: *What mass of magnesium oxide is produced when 60g of magnesium is burned in air?*

ANSWER:

1) *Write out the BALANCED EQUATION:*

$$2Mg + O_2 \rightarrow 2MgO$$

2) *Work out the RELATIVE FORMULA MASSES:*

(don't do the oxygen — we don't need it)

$$2 \times 24 \rightarrow 2 \times (24+16)$$
$$48 \rightarrow 80$$

3) Apply the rule: *DIVIDE TO GET ONE, THEN MULTIPLY TO GET ALL*

The two numbers, 48 and 80, tell us that *48g of Mg react to give 80g of MgO.*
Here's the 0 bit. You've now got to be able to write this down:

> 48g of Mg ......reacts to give.....80g of MgO
>
> 1g of Mg ......reacts to give.....
>
> 60g of Mg .....reacts to give......

THE BIG CLUE is that in the question they've said we want to burn *"60g of magnesium"*
i.e. they've told us how much *magnesium* to have, and that's how you know to write down the
LEFT HAND SIDE of it first, because:

We'll first need to ÷ by 48 to get 1g of Mg
and then need to × by 60 to get 60g of Mg.

THEN you can work out the numbers on the other side (shown in orange below) by realising
that you must *divide BOTH sides by 48* and then *multiply BOTH sides by 60*. It's tricky.

÷48 { 48g of Mg .... 80g of MgO } ÷48
      1g of Mg .... 1.67g of MgO
×60 { 60g of Mg .... 100g of MgO } ×60

You should realise that *in practise* 100% yield may not be obtained in some reactions, so the amount of product might be *slightly less than calculated.*

This finally tells us that *60g of magnesium will produce 100g of magnesium oxide.*
If the question had said "Find how much magnesium gives 500g of magnesium oxide.", you'd fill in the
MgO side first instead, *because that's the one you'd have the information about.* Got it? Good-O!

Reaction Mass Calculations? — no worries, matey...

Learn the three rules in the red box and practise the example till you can do it fluently.
1) Find the mass of calcium which gives 30g of calcium oxide (CaO), when burnt in air.

Calculating Volumes

These are OK as long as you *LEARN* the formula in the *RED BOX* and know how to use it.

1) Calculating the Volume *When you know the Masses*

For this type of question there are *TWO STAGES*:

1) *Find the reacting mass*, exactly like in the examples on the last page.

2) Then *convert the mass into a volume* using this formula:

$$\frac{VOL.\ OF\ GAS\ (in\ cm^3)}{24,000} = \frac{MASS\ OF\ GAS}{M_r\ of\ gas}$$

This formula comes from the well known(!) fact that:

A MASS OF M_r IN GRAMS, of any gas, will always occupy *24 LITRES* (at room temperature and pressure) — and it's the same for *ANY GAS*.

I reckon it's easier to learn and use the formula, but it's certainly worth knowing that fact too.

EXAMPLE: Find the volume of carbon dioxide produced (at room T and P) when 2.7g of carbon is
ANSWER: completely burned in oxygen. (A_r of carbon = 12, A_r of oxygen = 16)

1) Balanced equation: $C\ +\ O_2\ \rightarrow\ CO_2$

2) Fill in M_r for each: $\div12$ (12   32   44) $\div12$

3) Divide for one, times for all: $\times2.7$ (1 .... [3.6666667]) $\div12$
2.7 .... [9.8999999]) $\times2.7$
                                   = 9.9

4) So 2.7g of C gives 9.9g of CO_2.
   Now the new bit:

$$\frac{Volume}{24,000} = \frac{MASS}{M_r}$$

$$Volume = \frac{MASS}{M_r} \times 24,000$$

5) *USING THE ABOVE FORMULA:*

so Volume = $(MASS/M_r) \times 24,000$ = $(9.9/44) \times 24000$ = [5400.]

= 5400cm^3 or 5.40 litres

2) Calculating the Mass *when you're given the Volume*

For this type of question the *TWO STAGES* are in the *reverse order*:

1) First *find the mass from the volume* using the same formula as before:

$$\frac{VOL.\ OF\ GAS\ (in\ cm^3)}{24,000} = \frac{MASS\ OF\ GAS}{M_r\ of\ gas}$$

2) Then *find the reacting mass*, exactly like in the examples on the last page.

EXAMPLE: Find the mass of 6.2 litres of oxygen gas. (A_r of oxygen = 16)

ANSWER: Using the above formula: $\frac{6,200}{24,000} = \frac{Mass\ of\ Gas}{32}$

(Look out, 32, because it's O_2)

Hence,   Mass of Gas = $(6,200/24,000) \times 32$ = [8.2666667] = 8.27g

The question would likely go on to ask what mass of CO_2 would be produced if this much oxygen reacted with carbon. In that case you would now just apply the same old method from the previous page (as used above).

Calculating Volumes — it's just a gas...

Make sure you *learn the formula* in the red box at the top and that you know how to use it.
1) Find the volume of 2.5g of methane gas, CH_4, (at room T & P).
2) Find the mass of oxide (MgO) produced when magnesium is burned with 1.7 litres of oxygen.

Electrolysis Calculations

The important bit here is to get the balanced half equations, because they determine *THE RELATIVE AMOUNTS* of the two substances produced at the two electrodes. After that it's all the same as before, working out masses using M_r values, and volumes using the "M_r(g) = 24 litres" rule.

The Three Steps for Electrolysis Calculations

1) Write down the *TWO BALANCED HALF EQUATIONS*
   (i.e. match the number of electrons)
2) Write down the *BALANCED FORMULAE* for the
   two products obtained from the two electrodes.
3) *WRITE IN THE M_r VALUES* underneath each
   and carry on as for previous calculations.

EXAMPLE: In the electrolysis of sodium chloride, sodium is deposited at the cathode and chlorine gas is released at the anode. If 2.5g of sodium are collected at the cathode, find the volume of chlorine released.

ANSWER:

1) Balanced *half equations*:
$$2Na^+ + 2e^- \rightarrow 2Na$$
$$2Cl^- - 2e^- \rightarrow Cl_2$$

(2×23 because it's 2Na not just Na)

2) Balanced formulae of *products*:
   (as obtained from the balanced half equations)

3) Write in *M_r values*:
   ...and carry on as usual

(2×35.5 because it's Cl_2 not just Cl)

	2Na	Cl_2
	46	71

$\div46$ ⟨ 1 .... 1.5434782 ⟩ $\div46$

$\times2.5$ ⟨ 2.5 .... 3.8586956 ⟩ $\times2.5$

= **3.86**

So 2.5g of sodium will yield 3.86g of chlorine gas. Now we need this as a volume, so we use the good old *'mass to volume converting formula'*:

$$\text{Volume} = \frac{\text{MASS}}{24,000 \; M_r} \Rightarrow \text{Volume} = \frac{\text{MASS} \times 24,000}{M_r} = \frac{3.86 \times 24,000}{71} = \boxed{1304.3478}$$
$$= \underline{1304 \text{cm}^3}$$

And there it is, done in a flash. Just the same old stuff every time isn't it — balanced formulae, fill in M_r values, "divide and times" on both sides, and then use the "24,000 rule" to find the volume. Trivial.

Calculation of A_r from % abundances of Isotopes

Some elements, like chlorine, have A_r values which are not whole numbers. This is because there are *TWO STABLE ISOTOPES* of chlorine, ^{35}Cl and ^{37}Cl, and the mixture of the two gives an average A_r of 35.5. There is a simple formula for working out the overall A_r from the percentage abundances of two different isotopes:

$$\text{Overall } A_r = [(A_1 \times \%_{(1)}) + (A_2 \times \%_{(2)})] \div 100$$

FOR EXAMPLE if chlorine consists of 76% ^{35}Cl and 24% ^{37}Cl, then the overall value for A_r is:
Overall A_r = $[(35 \times 76) + (37 \times 24)] \div 100$ = 35.48 = $\underline{35.5}$ to 1 d.p.

Electrolysis — keep your hair on, it's not that bad...

With electrolysis calculations the main tricky bit is getting the balanced half equations right and then using the balanced symbol amounts for both products (e.g. 2Na and Cl_2).

1) In the electrolysis of aluminium oxide, Al_2O_3 if 23kg of aluminium is deposited at the cathode, what volume of oxygen will be liberated at the anode (when it's cooled down to room T and P anyway!)

Revision Summary for Section Three

Some more horrid questions to stress you out. The thing is though, why bother doing easy questions? These meaty monsters find out what you really know, and worse, what you really don't. Yeah, I know, it's kinda scary, but if you want to get anywhere in life you've got to face up to a bit of hardship. That's just the way it is. Take a few deep breaths and then try these:

(Answers on P. 90)

1)a) Describe each of these five types of chemical change: thermal decomposition, neutralisation, displacement, precipitation, reversible.
  b) Describe what is meant by an endothermic and an exothermic reaction.
  c) Describe what *reduction* and *oxidation* mean.
2) Give three rules for balancing equations. Balance these and put the state symbols in:
   a) $CaCO_3 + HCl \rightarrow CaCl_2 + H_2O + CO_2$ b) $Ca + H_2O \rightarrow Ca(OH)_2 + H_2$
   c) $H_2SO_4 + KOH \rightarrow K_2SO_4 + H_2O$ d) $Fe_2O_3 + H_2 \rightarrow Fe + H_2O$
   e) propane + oxygen $\rightarrow$ carbon dioxide + water
3) What is the rule for balancing half equations?
4) What are A_r and M_r?
5) What is the relationship between A_r and the number of protons and neutrons in the atom?
6) Find A_r or M_r for these (use the periodic table inside the front cover):
   a) Ca   b) Ag   c) CO_2 d) $MgCO_3$ e) Na_2CO_3 f) ZnO   g) KOH   h) NH_3
   i) butane   j) sodium chloride   k) Iron(II) chloride
7) What is the formula for calculating the percentage mass of an element in a compound?
   a) Calculate the percentage mass of oxygen in magnesium oxide, MgO
   b) Calculate the percentage mass of carbon in   i) $CaCO_3$ ii) CO_2 iii) Methane
   c) Calculate the percentage mass of metal in these oxides: i) Na_2O ii) Fe_2O_3 iii) Al_2O_3
8) What is meant by an empirical formula?
9) List the five steps of the method for finding an empirical formula (EF) from masses or %.
10) Work these out (using the periodic table):
   a) Find the EF for the iron oxide formed when 45.1g of iron reacts with 19.3g of oxygen.
   b) Find the EF for the compound formed when 227g of calcium reacts with 216g of fluorine.
   c) Find the EF for when 208.4g of carbon reacts with 41.7g of hydrogen.
   d) Find the EF when 21.9g of magnesium, 29.3g of sulphur and 58.4g of oxygen react.
11) Write down the three steps of the method for calculating reacting masses.
   a) What mass of magnesium oxide is produced when 112.1g of magnesium burns in air?
   b) What mass of sodium is needed to produce 108.2g of sodium oxide?
   c) What mass of carbon will react with hydrogen to produce 24.6g of propane?
12) What mass of gas occupies 24 litres at room temperature and pressure?
13) Write down the formula for calculating the volume of a known mass of gas (at room T & P).
   a) What is the volume of 56.0g of nitrogen at room T & P?
   b) Find the volume of carbon dioxide produced when 5.6g of carbon is completely burned.
   c) What volume of oxygen will react with 25.0g of hydrogen to produce water?
   d) What is the mass of 5.4 litres of nitrogen gas?
   e) What mass of carbon dioxide is produced when 4.7 litres of oxygen reacts with carbon?
14) Write down the three steps for electrolysis calculations.
   a) In the electrolysis of NaCl, find the mass of Cl_2 released if 3.4g of sodium are collected.
   b) In the electrolysis of copper(II) chloride, what volume of chlorine gas would be produced for every 100g of copper obtained?
15) Why do some elements, such as chlorine and rubidium, have A_r values that are not whole numbers?

Atmospheric Problems

Don't confuse these two different atmospheric problems. They're all _totally separate!_
(The Biology Book has more details on these. Well, it has more space for pretty pictures anyway.)

1) Acid Rain is caused by Sulphur Dioxide and Nitrogen Oxides

1) When _fossil fuels_ are burned they release _mostly_ CO_2 (which causes the Greenhouse Effect).
2) But they also release _two_ other harmful gases, _sulphur dioxide_ and various _nitrogen oxides_.
3) The sulphur dioxide, SO_2, comes from sulphur _impurities_ in the _fossil fuels_.
4) However, the _nitrogen oxides_ are created from a reaction between the nitrogen and oxygen in the air, caused by the _heat_ of the burning.
5) When these gases _mix_ with clouds they form dilute _sulphuric acid_ and dilute _nitric acid_.
6) This then falls as _acid rain_.
7) _Cars_ and _power stations_ are the main causes of acid rain.

Acid Rain Kills Fish, Trees and Statues

1) _Acid rain_ causes _lakes_ to become _acidic_ and many plants and animals _die_ as a result.
2) Acid rain kills _trees_ and damages _limestone_ buildings and ruins _stone statues_. It's shocking.

2) The Greenhouse Effect is caused by CO_2 trapping heat

1) The _Greenhouse Effect_ is causing the Earth to _warm up_ very slowly.
2) It's caused mainly by a rise in the level of CO_2 in the atmosphere due to the _burning_ of massive amounts of _fossil fuels_ in the last two hundred years or so.
3) The _carbon dioxide_ (and a few other gases) _trap_ the heat that reaches Earth from the sun.
4) This will cause a _rise_ in _temperature_ which is then likely to cause changes in _climate_ and weather patterns all over the world and possible _flooding_ due to the _polar ice caps_ _melting_.
5) The _level of CO2_ in the atmosphere has _gone up_ by about _20%_, and will _continue to rise_ as long as we keep burning _fossil fuels_, as the graph clearly shows.
6) _Deforestation_ is not helping either.
7) The increased concentration of CO_2 in the atmosphere means the _ocean surfaces_ absorb a bit more CO_2, but not enough to stop the rising levels.

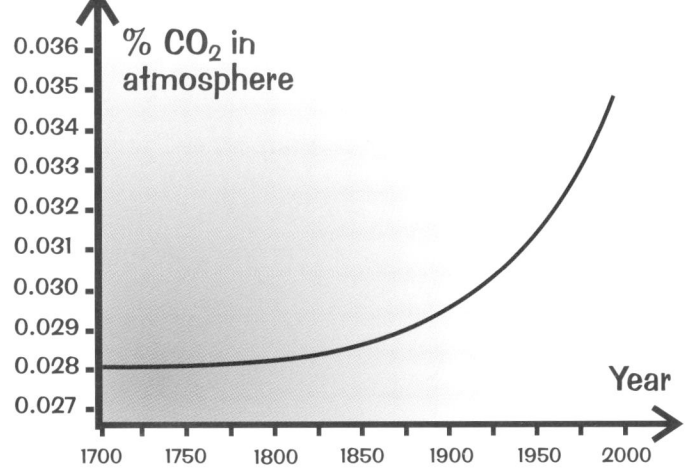

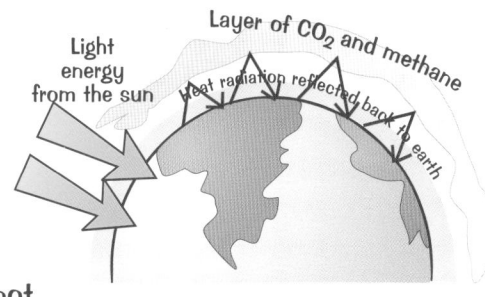

Eee, problems, problems — there's always summat goin' wrong...

It's a bit surprising just how much stuff there is on these environmental problems, but I'm afraid there's plenty of past Exam questions which ask precisely these details. If you want those marks, you've gotta learn these drivelly facts, and that's that. _You know the drill_: _learn, cover, scribble, check... learn..._

The Evolution of the Atmosphere

The present composition of the atmosphere is: _78% Nitrogen_, _21% oxygen_, _0.04% CO_2_ (= 99.04%). The remaining 1% is made up of noble gases (mainly argon). In addition there can be a lot of water vapour. But the atmosphere wasn't _always_ like this. Here's how the first 4.5 billion years have gone:

Phase 1 — Volcanoes gave out Steam, CO_2, NH_3 and CH_4

1) The Earth's surface was originally _molten_ for many millions of years. Any atmosphere _boiled away_.
2) Eventually it cooled and a thin crust formed but _volcanoes_ kept erupting.
3) They belched out mostly _carbon dioxide_.
4) But also some _steam_, _ammonia_ and _methane_.
5) The early atmosphere was _mostly_ CO_2.
6) There was virtually _no_ oxygen.
7) The water vapour _condensed_ to form the _oceans_.
8) _Holiday report_: Not a nice place to be. Take strong walking boots and a good coat.

Phase 2 — Green Plants Evolved and produced Oxygen

1) Green _plants_ evolved over most of the Earth.
2) They were quite happy in the _CO_2 atmosphere_.
3) A lot of the early CO_2 _dissolved_ into the oceans.
4) But the green plants steadily _removed_ CO_2 and _produced_ O_2.
5) Much of the CO_2 from the air thus became locked up in _fossil fuels_ and _sedimentary rocks_.
6) _Methane_ and _ammonia_ reacted with the _oxygen_, releasing _nitrogen_ gas.
7) Ammonia was also converted into _nitrates_ by nitrifying bacteria.
8) _Nitrogen_ gas was also released by _living organisms_ like denitrifying bacteria.
9) _Holiday Report_: A bit slimy underfoot. Take wellies and a lot of suncream.

Phase 3 — Ozone Layer allows Evolution of Complex Animals

1) The build-up of _oxygen_ in the atmosphere _killed off_ early organisms that couldn't tolerate it.
2) It also enabled the _evolution_ of more _complex_ organisms that made use of the oxygen.
3) The oxygen also created the _ozone layer_ (O_3) which _blocked_ harmful rays from the sun and _enabled_ even more _complex_ organisms to evolve.
4) There is virtually _no CO_2_ left now.
5) _Holiday report_: A nice place to be. Get there before the crowds ruin it.

Coo... 4½ Billion Years — just takes your breath away...

I think it's pretty amazing how much the atmosphere has changed. It makes our present day obsession about the CO_2 going up from 0.03% to 0.04% seem a bit ridiculous, doesn't it!
Anyway, never mind that, just _learn the three phases with all their details_. You don't have to draw the diagrams — although thinking about it, it's a pretty good way to remember it all, don't you think. Yip.

Today's Atmosphere and Oceans

The atmosphere we have today is _just right_.
It has _gradually_ evolved over billions of years and _we_ have evolved with it. All very slowly.
We worry that we're changing it _for the worse_ by releasing various gases from _industrial activity_.
Two of the biggest worries are _The Greenhouse Effect_ and _Acid Rain_.
These are described on the previous pages. (And in more detail in the Biology Book.)

Composition of _Today's_ Atmosphere

Present composition of the atmosphere:

78%	Nitrogen
1%	Argon
21%	Oxygen
0.04%	Carbon dioxide

(Often written as 79% Nitrogen for simplicity.)

(That comes to over 100% because the first three are rounded up very slightly)

Also :
1) Varying amounts of _WATER VAPOUR_.
2) And other _noble gases_ in very small amounts.

A Simple Experiment to find the % of Oxygen in the Air

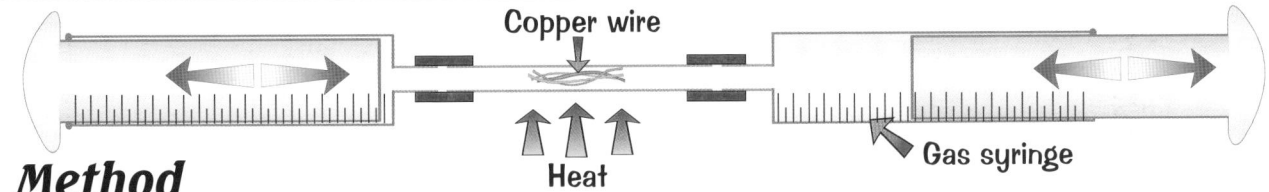

Copper wire

Heat

Gas syringe

Method

1) Measure the _initial volume_ of air, then push it back and forth over the _heated copper_.
2) The copper _takes out_ the oxygen and produces _black copper oxide_.
3) When no more copper is turning black, let it _cool_ and measure the _amount_ of air left.
4) As a _check_, _heat_ the copper _again_ for a while, cool and _measure_ the volume again.
5) Then _calculate_:

$$\text{Percentage of oxygen} = \frac{\text{Change in volume} \times 100}{\text{Original volume}}$$

The Oceans Hold a lot of Carbon

1) The _Oceans_ were formed by _condensation_ of the _steam_ in the early atmosphere.
2) They then started absorbing the _CO_2_ from the atmosphere.
3) They now contain a _large_ amount of carbon in _three_ main forms:
   a) Carbon dioxide _dissolved_ in the water
   b) _Insoluble carbonates_ like calcium carbonate (shells, which form sediment and then limestone)
   c) _Soluble compounds_ like hydrogen-carbonates of Ca, Mg

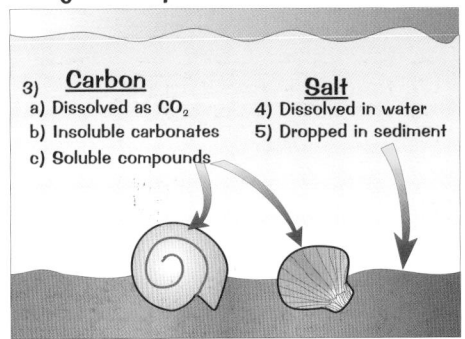

3)   Carbon
a) Dissolved as CO_2
b) Insoluble carbonates
c) Soluble compounds

      Salt
4) Dissolved in water
5) Dropped in sediment

4) The Oceans are gradually getting _saltier_.
5) Some salts are removed by various _chemical_ and _biological_ processes and dropped as _sediment_.
6) This eventually turns into _rocks_ and these eventually _wash back in again_ millions of years later.

Less than 1% water vapour? — so how come it's always raining...

This is all pretty simple. It's the kinda stuff that some of you might have thought doesn't need to be learnt.   Tut tut tut tut tut tut. You should know better than that — d'ya really think I'd waste one of my precious pages on irrelevant junk?   Nope. No way. _So learn it_.

The Three Different Types of Rocks

Rocks shouldn't be confusing. There are _three_ different types: _sedimentary_, _metamorphic_ and _igneous_.
Over _millions_ of years they _change_ from one into another.   This is called the _Rock Cycle_.   Astonishingly.

The Rock Cycle

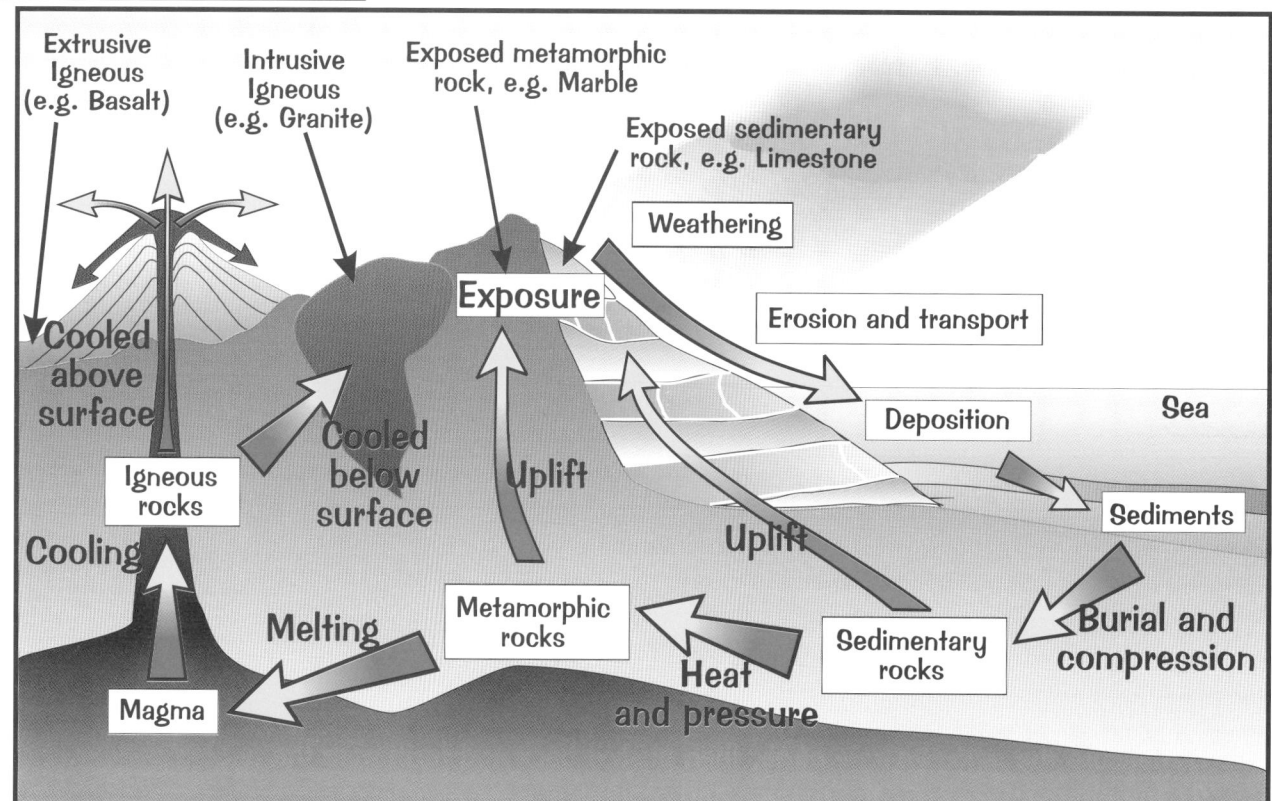

The Rocks Change from One to Another in a Slow Cycle

1) Particles get washed to the _sea_ and settle as _sediment_.
2) Over _millions_ of years these sediments get _crushed_ into **SEDIMENTARY** rocks (hence the name).
3) At first they get _buried_, but they can either _rise_ to the surface again to be discovered, or they can _descend_ into the _heat_ and _pressure_ below.
4) If they _do_, the heat and pressure _completely alter_ the structure of the rock and they then become **METAMORPHIC ROCKS**   (as in "metamorphosis" or "change". Another good name!).
5) These _metamorphic rocks_ can either rise to the _surface_ to be discovered by an enthusiastic geologist or else descend _still further_ into the fiery abyss of the Earth's raging inferno where they will _melt_ and become _magma_.
6) When _magma_ reaches the surface it _cools_ and _sets_ and is then called **IGNEOUS ROCK**.
    ("igneous" as in "ignite" or "fire" — another cool name. Gee, if only biology names were this sensible.)
7) There are actually _two types_ of igneous rock:
    1) **EXTRUSIVE** when it comes _straight out_ of the surface from a _volcano_ ("Ex-" as in "Exit").
    2) **INTRUSIVE** when it just sets as a big lump _below_ the surface ("In-" as in "inside")
        (I have to say — whoever invented these names deserves a medal)
8) When any of these rocks reach the _surface_, then _weathering_ begins and they gradually get _worn down_ and carried off to the _sea_ and the whole cycle _starts over again_...   Simple, innit?

Rocks are a mystery — no, no, it's sedimentary my Dear Watson...

Don't you think the Rock Cycle is pretty ace? Can you think of anything you'd rather do than go on a family holiday to Cornwall, gazing at the cliffs and marvelling at the different types of rocks and stuff? Exactly.   (And even if you can, it's still a good plan to _learn about rocks_.)

Sedimentary Rocks

Three steps in the Formation of Sedimentary Rocks

1) _Sedimentary rocks_ are formed from _layers of sediment_ laid down in _lakes_ or _seas_.
2) Over _millions of years_ the layers get buried under more layers and the _weight_ pressing down _squeezes_ out the water.
3) As the water disappears, _salts_ crystallize out and _cement_ the particles together.

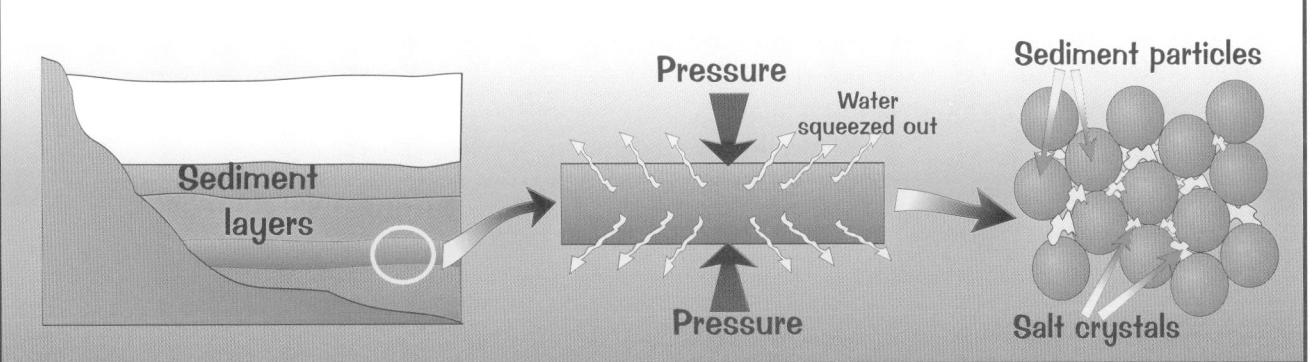

Fossils are only found in Sedimentary Rocks

1) Only _sedimentary_ rocks contain _fossils_. The other two types of rock, metamorphic and igneous, have been through too much _heat and trauma_ to have fossils left in them.
2) Sedimentary rocks have only been _gently crushed_ for a few million years. No big deal, so the fossils _survive_. All sedimentary rocks are likely to contain fossils.
3) Fossils are a very useful way of _identifying rocks_ as being of the _same age_.
4) This is because fossilised remains that are found _change_ (due to evolution) as the _ages pass_.
5) This means that if two rocks have the _same fossils_ they must be from the _same age_.
6) However, if the fossils in two rocks are _different_, it proves _nothing_ don't forget!

The Four Main Sedimentary Rocks:

Sedimentary rocks tend to look similar to the _original sediments_ from which they formed. After all, _very little_ has happened other than them _squashing_ together.

1) Sandstone

This is formed from _sand_ of course. And it looks like it too. Sandstone just looks like _sand particles_ all stuck very firmly together. There's _red_ sandstone and _yellow_ sandstone which are commonly used for _buildings_. The now famous Barrow Town Hall is built in red sandstone.

2) Limestone

This formed from _seashells_. It's mostly _calcium carbonate_ and _grey/white_ in colour. The original _shells_ are mostly _crushed_ but there are still quite a few _fossilised shells_ to be found in _limestone_.

3) Mudstone or shale

This was formed from _mud_ which basically means _finer_ particles than _sand_.
It's often _dark grey_ and tends to _split_ into the _original layers_ very easily.

4) Conglomerates

These look like a sort of crude _concrete_, containing _pebbles_ set into a _cement_ of finer particles.

Revision Pressure — don't get crushed by it...

Quite a lot of facts here on sedimentary rocks. You've gotta _learn_ how they form, that they contain fossils, and also the names etc. of the four examples. Most important you need to be able to _describe_ in words _what they all look like_. Even if you don't really know, just learn the descriptions!

Metamorphic Rocks

Heat and Pressure over Thousands of Years

Metamorphic rocks are formed by the action of _heat_ and _pressure_ on existing (_sedimentary_) rocks over _long_ periods of time.

1) _Earth movements_ can push all types of rock _deep_ underground.

2) Here they are compressed and heated, and the _mineral structure_ and _texture_ may change.

3) So long as they don't actually _melt_ they are classed as _metamorphic_ rocks.

4) _If they melt_ and turn to _magma_, they're _gone_. The magma may resurface as igneous rocks.

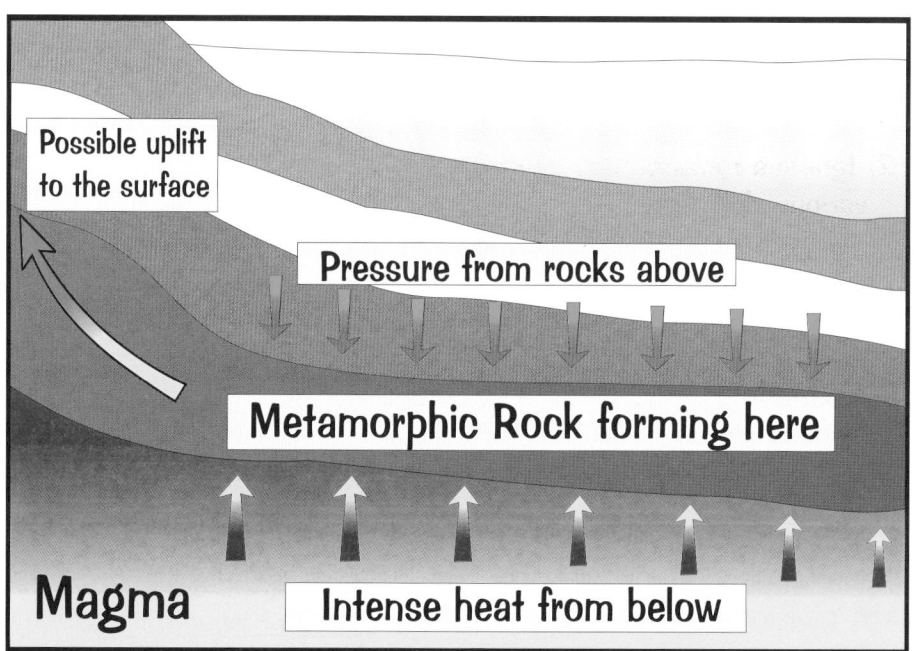

Possible uplift to the surface

Pressure from rocks above

Metamorphic Rock forming here

Magma

Intense heat from below

Slate, Marble and Schist are Metamorphic Rocks

1) Slate is formed from mudstone or clay

1) As the mudstone gets _heated_ and _compressed_ its tiny _plate-like_ particles align in the _same direction_.
2) This allows the resulting _slate_ to be _split_ along that direction into _thin sheets_ which make _ideal_ roofing material.
3) The increasingly famous Barrow Town Hall has a slate roof.

2) Marble is formed from Limestone

1) Very high temperature will break down the _shells_ in limestone and they reform as _small crystals_.
2) This gives marble a _more even texture_ and makes it much _harder_.
3) It can be _polished up_ and often has attractive patterning.
4) This makes it a great _decorative stone_. My Uncle Cyril has a fabulous Marble Headstone.

3) Schist is Formed when Mudstone gets real hot

1) Mudstone will turn to slate only if there's plenty of pressure but _not_ too much heat.
2) If mudstone gets _really_ hot, _new minerals_ like _mica_ start to form and create _layers_.
3) This creates _Schist_, a rock containing _bands of interlocking crystals_.
4) These layers of crystals are typical of a _metamorphic_ rock.
5) Only _steady_ heat and pressure will cause this to happen.

Schist! — when the heat and pressure is all too much...

There's quite a lot of names accumulating now. Somehow, you've got to make sense of them in your head. It really does help _if you know what these rocks actually look like_ in real life.

It's best if you can think of specific objects made of them. Otherwise, it'll all get pretty tricky.

Igneous Rocks

Igneous Rocks are formed from Fresh Magma

1) _Igneous rocks_ form when _molten_ magma pushes up into the _crust_ or right _through it_.

2) Igneous rocks contain various different _minerals_ in _randomly_-arranged interlocking _crystals_.

3) There are _two types_ of igneous rocks: _EXTRUSIVE_ and _INTRUSIVE_:

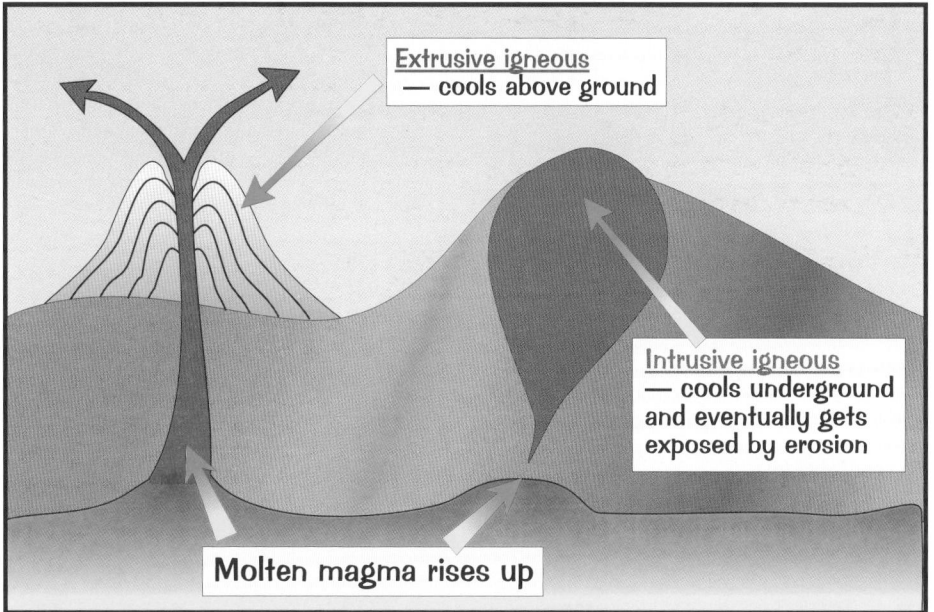

Extrusive igneous — cools above ground

Intrusive igneous — cools underground and eventually gets exposed by erosion

Molten magma rises up

INTRUSIVE igneous rocks cool SLOWLY with BIG crystals

GRANITE is an intrusive igneous rock with big crystals

1) _Granite_ is formed _underground_ where the magma cools down _slowly_.
2) This means it has _big_ randomly-arranged _crystals_ because it cools down _slowly_.
3) Granite is a very _hard_ and _decorative_ stone ideal for steps and buildings.
4) Barrow Town Hall? Don't know.

EXTRUSIVE igneous rocks cool QUICKLY with SMALL crystals

BASALT is an extrusive igneous rock with small crystals

1) _Basalt_ is formed _on top_ of the Earth's crust after _bursting out_ of a _volcano_.
2) This means it has _relatively small_ crystals — because it _cooled quickly_.

Identifying Rocks in Exam Questions

A typical question will simply _describe_ a rock and ask you to _identify it_. Make sure you learn the information on rocks well enough to work _backwards_, as it were, so that you can _identify_ the type of rock from a description. _Practise_ by doing these:

Rock A: Small crystals in layers.
Rock B: Contains fossils.
Rock C: Randomly arranged crystals of various types.
Rock D: Hard, smooth and with wavy layers of crystals.
Rock E: Large crystals. Very hard wearing.
Rock F: Sandy texture. Fairly soft.

Answers
A: _metamorphic_
B: _sedimentary_
C: _igneous_
D: _metamorphic_
E: _Igneous (granite)_
F: _Sedimentary (sandstone)_

Igneous Rocks are real cool — or they're magma...

It's very important that you know what granite looks like. You really should insist that "Teach" organises a field trip to see the famous pink granite coast of Brittany. About two weeks should be enough time to fully appreciate it. In May. Failing that, sit and _learn this page_ in cold grey Britain for ten minutes.

The Earth's Structure

Crust, Mantle, Outer and Inner Core

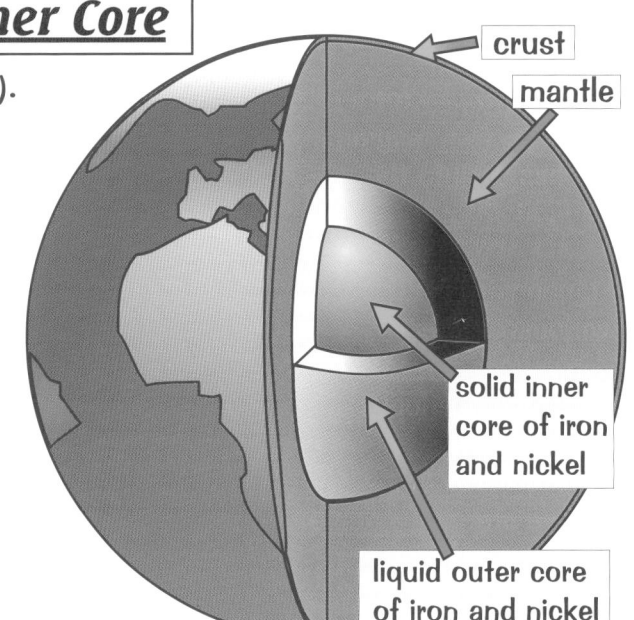

1) The _crust_ is very _thin_ (well, about 20km or so!).
2) The _mantle_ is _liquid_ but very _viscous_.
3) The _core_ is just over _half_ the Earth's radius.
4) The _core_ is made from _iron_ and _nickel_. This is where the Earth's _magnetic field_ originates.
5) The iron and nickel _sank_ to the "bottom" long ago (i.e. the centre of the Earth) because they're _denser_.
6) The core has a _solid inner_ bit and a _liquid outer_ bit.
7) _Radioactive decay_ creates all the _heat_ inside the Earth.
8) This heat causes the _convection currents_ which cause the plates of the crust to move.

crust

mantle

solid inner core of iron and nickel

liquid outer core of iron and nickel

Big Clues: Seismic Waves, Magnetism and Meteorites

1) The overall _density_ of the Earth is much _higher_ than the density of _rock_. This means the _inside_ must be made of something _denser_ than rock.
2) _Meteorites_ which crash to Earth are often made of _iron_ and _nickel_.
3) Iron and nickel are both _magnetic_ and very _dense_.
4) So if the _CORE_ of the Earth were made of iron and nickel it would explain a lot, i.e. the _high density_ of the Earth and the fact that it has a magnetic field round it (see the Physics Book).
5) Also, by following the paths of _seismic waves_ from earthquakes as they travel through the Earth, we can tell that there is a _change_ to _liquid_ about _halfway_ through the Earth.
6) Hence we deduce a _liquid outer core_ of iron and nickel. The seismic waves also indicate a solid inner core (refer to the Physics Book). See how very easy it all is when you know.

The Earth's Surface is made up of Large Plates of Rock

1) These _plates_ are like _big rafts_ that float across the liquid mantle.
2) The map shows the _edges_ of these plates. As they _move_, the _continents_ move too.
3) The plates are moving at a speed of about 1cm or 2cm _per year_.

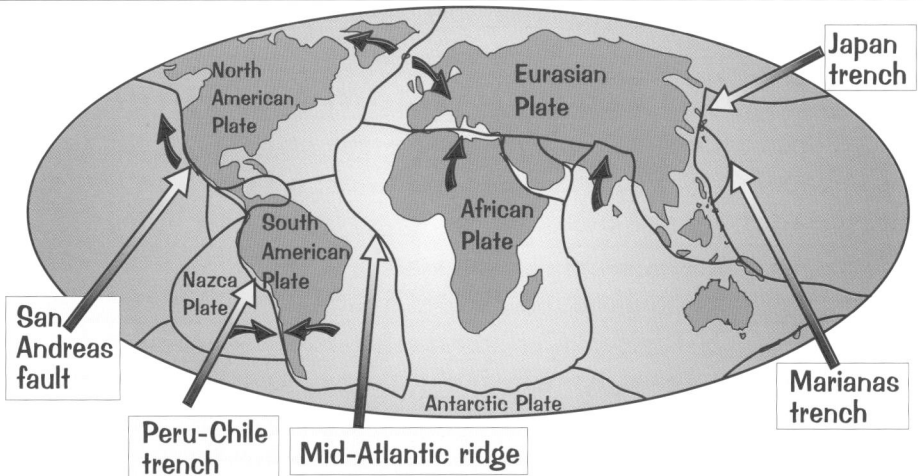

North American Plate
Eurasian Plate
Japan trench
African Plate
South American Plate
Nazca Plate
San Andreas fault
Antarctic Plate
Marianas trench
Peru-Chile trench
Mid-Atlantic ridge

Try Telling that lot to the Spanish Inquisition...

More _nice easy stuff_. That means it's nice easy marks in the Exam too. They do put easy stuff in, just so that everyone gets at least some marks. Just make sure you learn _ALL_ the details. There's _nothing dafter_ than missing easy marks. _Cover the page and check you know it ALL._

Evidence for Plate Tectonics

Crinkly bits from Cooling? — I don't think so, matey

The old theory was that all the _features_ of the Earth's surface, e.g. mountains, were due to _shrinkage_ of the crust as it _cooled_. In the Exam they may well ask you about that, and then they'll ask you for _evidence_ in favour of _plate tectonics_ as a _better theory_. Learn and prosper:

1) Jigsaw Fit — the supercontinent "Pangaea"

a) There's a very obvious _jigsaw fit_ between _Africa_ and _South America_.
b) The _other_ continents can also be fitted in without too much trouble.
c) It's widely believed that they once all formed a _single_ land mass, now called _Pangaea_.

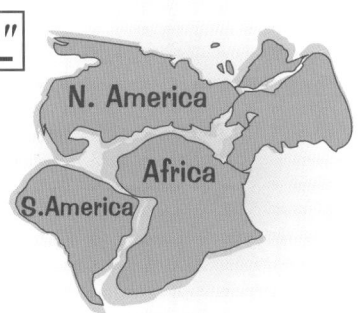

2) Matching Fossils in Africa and South America

a) Identical _plant fossils_ of the _same age_ have been found in rocks in _South Africa_, _Australia_, _Antarctica_, _India_ and _South America_, which strongly suggests they were all _joined_ once upon a time.
b) _Animal fossils_ support the theory too. There are identical fossils of a freshwater _crocodile_ found in both _Brazil_ and _South Africa_. It certainly didn't swim across.

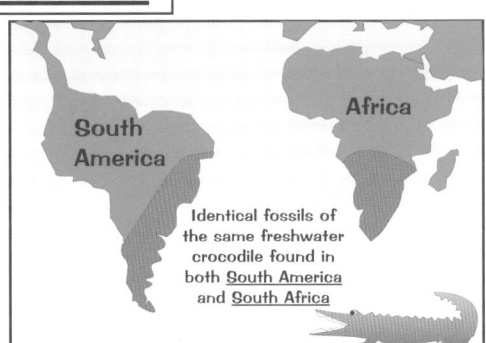

Identical fossils of the same freshwater crocodile found in both South America and South Africa

3) Living Creatures: The Earthworm

a) There are various living creatures found in _both_ America and Africa.
b) One such beasty is a particular _earthworm_ which is found living at the tip of _South America_ and the tip of _South Africa_.
c) How come? Well most likely it travelled across _ever so slowly_ on the big raft we now call America.

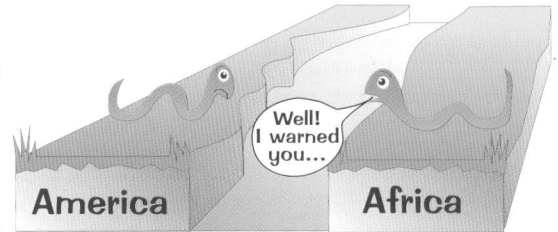

Well! I warned you...

America   Africa

4) Identical Rock Sequences

a) When _rock strata_ of similar _ages_ are studied in various countries they show remarkable _similarity_.
b) This is strong evidence that these countries were _joined together_ when the rocks _formed_.

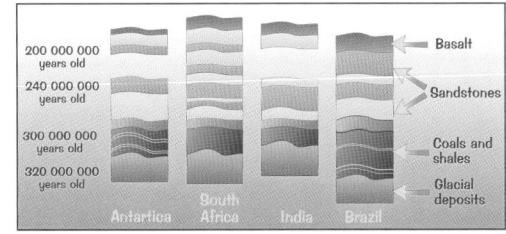

5) Magnetic Stripes in the Ocean Floor

(See P. 49 for fuller details on this)

a) The _symmetrical pattern_ of _magnetic "stripes"_ in the rocks on either side of the _Mid-Atlantic ridge_ is the clearest evidence of all that the two sides are _spreading_ away from each other.
b) These magnetic stripes were only discovered in the 1960s.

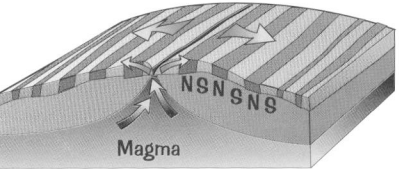

Learn about Plate Tectonics — but don't get carried away...

Five bits of evidence which support the theory that there are big plates of rock moving about. Learn all five well enough to be able to answer a question like this: "Describe evidence which supports the theory of Plate Tectonics" (5 marks). _Learn, cover, scribble, etc..._

Plate Boundaries

At the _boundaries_ between tectonic plates there's usually trouble like _volcanoes_ or _earthquakes_. There are _three_ different ways that plates interact: _Colliding_, _separating_ or _sliding_ past each other.

Plates Sliding Past Each Other: San Francisco

1) Sometimes the plates are just _sliding_ past each other.
2) The best known example of this is the _San Andreas Fault_ in California.
3) A narrow strip of the coastline is sliding north at about _7cm a year_.
4) Big plates of rock _don't glide smoothly_ past each other.
5) They _catch_ on each other and as the _forces build up_ they suddenly _lurch_.
6) This _sudden lurching_ only lasts _a few seconds_ — but it'll bring buildings down, no problem.
7) The city of _San Francisco_ sits _astride_ this fault line. (They didn't know that when they built it!)
8) The city was _destroyed_ by an earthquake in _1906_ and hit by another quite serious one in _1991_. They could have another one any time.
9) In _earthquake zones_ they try to build _earthquake-proof_ buildings which are designed to withstand a bit of shaking.
10) Earthquakes usually cause _much greater devastation_ in _poorer countries_ where they may have _overcrowded cities_, _poorly constructed buildings_, and _inadequate rescue services_.

Oceanic and Continental Plates Colliding: The Andes

1) The _oceanic_ plate is always forced _underneath_ the continental plate.
2) This is called a _subduction zone_.
3) As the oceanic crust is pushed down it _melts_ and _pressure_ builds up due to all the melting rock.
4) This _molten rock_ finds its way to the surface and _volcanoes_ form.
5) There are also _earthquakes_ as the two plates slowly _grind_ past each other.
6) A deep _trench_ forms on the ocean floor where the _oceanic plate_ is being _forced_ down.
7) The _continental_ crust _crumples_ and _folds_ forming _mountains_ at the coast.
8) The classic example of all this is the west coast of _South America_ where the _Andes mountains_ are. That region has _all_ the features:

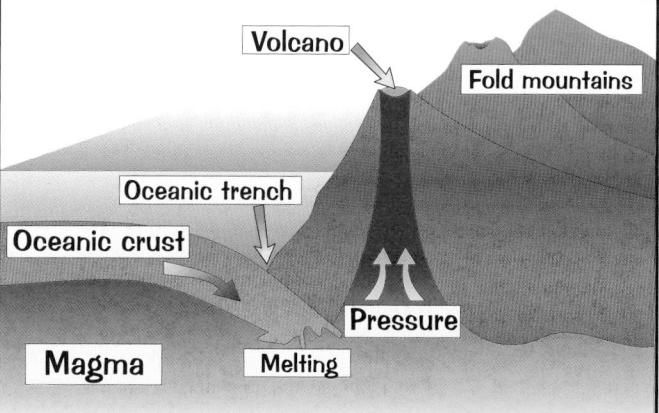

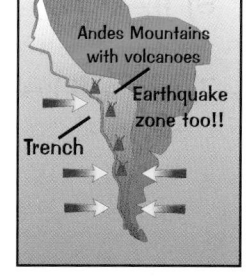

Volcanoes, _earthquakes_, an _oceanic trench_ and _mountains_.

Another page to learn — don't make a mountain out of it...

Make sure you learn all these diagrams — they summarise all the information in the text. They may well ask you for examples in the Exam, so make sure you know the two different kinds of situation that the Andes and San Francisco actually represent. _Cover and scribble..._

Plate Boundaries

Sea Floor Spreading 1: The mid-Atlantic Ridge

1) When tectonic plates move apart, _magma_ rises up to fill the gap and produces _new crust_ made of _basalt_ (of course). Sometimes it comes out with great _force_ producing _undersea volcanoes_.

2) The _Mid-Atlantic ridge_ runs the whole length of the Atlantic and actually cuts through the middle of _Iceland_, which is why they have _hot underground water_.

3) Earthquakes and volcanoes under the sea can cause massive _tidal waves (tsunami)_. These waves can cause great destruction when they reach land.

4) As the magma rises up through the gap it forms _ridges_ and _underwater mountains_.

5) These form a _symmetrical pattern_ either side of the ridge, providing strong _evidence_ for the theory of _continental drift_.

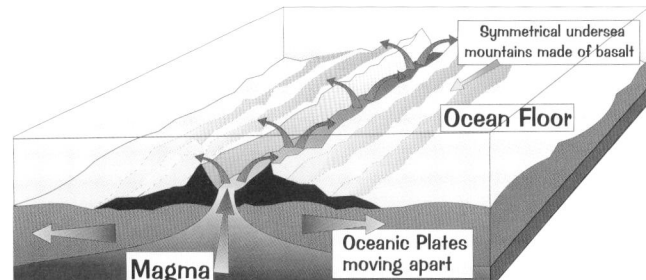
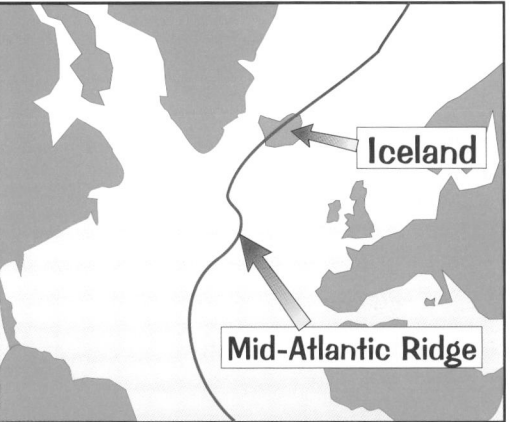

Sea Floor Spreading 2: Magnetic Reversal Patterns

1) However the most compelling evidence in favour of continental drift comes from the _magnetic orientation_ of the rocks.

2) As the _liquid magma_ erupts out of the gap, the _iron particles_ in the rocks tend to _align themselves_ with the _Earth's magnetic field_ and as it cools they _set_ in position.

3) Every half million years or so the Earth's magnetic field tends to _swap direction_.

4) This means the rock on _either side of the ridge_ has bands of _alternate_ magnetic polarity.

5) This pattern is found to be _symmetrical_ either side of the ridge.

6) These magnetic stripes were _only_ discovered in the _1960's_.

7) These stripes spread out at a rate of about _2 cm per year_, which is pretty slow. In fact, continents move at pretty much the same speed your fingernails grow at. It's sad, but you probably _won't_ observe any continental drift in your lifetime!

Sea Floor Spreading — Learn the Shocking Truth...

Another couple of bits of evidence which support the theory that there are big plates of rock moving about. Learn all five well enough to be able to answer a question like this: "Describe evidence which supports the theory of Plate Tectonics" (5 marks). _Learn, cover, scribble, etc..._

Revision Summary For Section Four

Well let's face it, this section on Air and Rock is definitely the easy interlude in the Chemistry syllabus. In the Olden Days (the 1970's) this stuff all used to be called Geography, which as you know, is a much easier subject than Chemistry. However, easy or not, there's still quite a lot of stuff to learn. Try these little jokers and see how much you know:

1) Name two man-made atmospheric problems.
2) Which gases cause acid rain? Where do they come from?
3) What are the three adverse effects of acid rain?
4) Which gas causes the Greenhouse effect? Explain how the Greenhouse effect works.
5) How old is the Earth? What was it like for the first billion years or so?
6) What gases did the early atmosphere consist of? Where did these gases come from?
7) What was the main thing which caused phase two of the atmosphere's evolution?
8) Which gases became much less common and which one increased?
9) Which gas allowed phase three to take place?
10) Which gas is almost completely gone?
11) What are the percentages of gases in today's atmosphere?
12) Describe a simple experiment to find the percentage of oxygen in air.
13) What is the formula used to calculate the percentage of oxygen in the air, from experiment?
14) How did the oceans form?
15) Explain the three ways in which the oceans contain carbon, and two ways they contain salt.
16) What are the three types of rock? Draw a full diagram of the rock cycle.
17) Explain how the three types of rock change from one to another. How long does this take?
18) Draw diagrams to show how sedimentary rocks form.
19) How and why can fossils be used to identify rocks as being the same age?
20) What are found in sedimentary rocks but are not found in any other type of rock?
21) List the four main sedimentary rocks, give a description of each, and a use for two of them.
22) Draw a diagram to show how metamorphic rocks are formed. What does the name mean?
23) What are the three main metamorphic rocks?
24) Describe their appearance and give a use for two of them.
25) Describe how the three main metaphoric rocks are formed.
26) How are igneous rocks formed? What are the two types? Give an example of each.
27) What is the difference in the way that they formed and in their structure and appearance?
28) Draw a diagram of the internal structure of the Earth, with labels.
29) How big are the various parts in relation to each other? What is the mantle made of?
30) What is the core made of? What are the three big clues that tell us about the Earth?
31) What was the old theory about the Earth's surface? What is the theory of Plate Tectonics?
32) Give details of the five bits of evidence which support the theory of Plate Tectonics.
33) What are the three different ways that tectonic plates interact at boundaries?
34) Where is the San Andreas fault? What are the tectonic plates doing along this fault line?
35) Why does it cause Earthquakes — and why did they build San Francisco right on top of it?
36) What happens when two continental plates collide? Draw diagrams.
37) What features does this produce? Which part of the world is the classic case of this?
38) What happens when an oceanic plate collides with a continental plate? Draw a diagram.
39) What four features does this produce? Which part of the world is the classic case of this?
40) What is the mid-Atlantic ridge? What happens there?
41) Which country lies on top of it? Do they suffer Earthquakes? What *do* they get?
42) How were magnetic reversal patterns formed?
43) Why do magnetic reversal patterns provide us with good evidence of continental drift?

A History of The Periodic Table

Periodic Table

The early Chemists were keen to try and find _patterns_ in the elements.
The more elements that were identified, the easier it became to find patterns of course.

In the Early 1800s They Could Only go on Atomic Mass

They had _two_ obvious ways to categorise elements:

1) Their _physical_ and _chemical_ properties	2) Their _Relative Atomic Mass_

1) Remember, they had _no idea_ of _atomic structure_ or of protons or electrons, so there was _no_ such thing
as _proton number_ to them. (It was only in the 20th Century after protons and electrons were
discovered, that it was realised the elements should be arranged in order of _proton number_.)
2) But back then, the only thing they could measure was _Relative Atomic Mass_ and the only obvious way
to arrange the known elements was in order of _atomic mass_.
3) When this was done a _periodic pattern_ was noticed in the _properties_ of the elements.

Newlands' Octaves Were The First Good Effort

A chap called _Newlands_ had the first good stab at it in _1863_. He noticed that every _eighth_ element had
similar properties and so he listed some of the known elements in rows of seven:

Li	Be	B	C	N	O	F
Na	Mg	Al	Si	P	S	Cl

These sets of eight were called _Newlands' Octaves_ but unfortunately the pattern _broke down_ on the _third
row_ with many _transition metals_ like Fe and Cu and Zn messing it up completely.
It was because he left _no_ gaps that his work was _ignored_.
But he was getting _pretty close_, as you can see.

Dmitri Mendeleev Left Gaps and Predicted New Elements

1) In _1869_, _Dmitri Mendeleev_ in Russia, armed with about 50 known elements, arranged them
into his Table of Elements with various _gaps_, as shown.
2) Mendeleev ordered the elements in order of _atomic mass_ (like Newlands did).
3) But Mendeleev found he had to leave _gaps_ in order to keep elements with _similar properties_ in
the same _vertical groups_ — and he was prepared to leave some very _big_ gaps in the first two
rows before the transition metals come in on the _third_ row.

The _gaps_ were the really clever
bit because they _predicted_ the
properties of so far
undiscovered elements.

When they were found and
they _fitted_ the pattern it was
pretty smashing news for old
Dmitri. The old rogue.

Mendeleev's Table of the Elements

H																		
Li	Be													B	C	N	O	F
Na	Mg													Al	Si	P	S	Cl
K	Ca	*		Ti	V	Cr	Mn	Fe	Co	Ni	Cu	Zn	*	*	As	Se	Br	
Rb	Sr	Y		Zr	Nb	Mo	*	Ru	Rh	Pd	Ag	Cd	In	Sn	Sb	Te	I	
Cs	Ba	*	*	Ta	W	*	Os	Ir	Pt	Au	Hg	Tl	Pb	Bi				

I Can't see what all the fuss is — it all seems quite elementary...

They're quite into having bits of History in Science now. They like to think you'll gain an appreciation of
the role of science in the overall progress of human society. Personally, I'm not that bothered whether
you do or not. All I wanna know is: _Have you learnt all the facts yet?_ And if not — _WHY NOT? HUH?_

The Periodic Table

Group O

| 1 H Hydrogen 1 | | | | | | | | | | | | | | | | | | 4 He Helium 2 |

Group I — Group II ... Group III — Group IV — Group V — Group VI — Group VII

Period	Group I	Group II											Group III	Group IV	Group V	Group VI	Group VII	Group O
2	7 Li Lithium 3	9 Be Beryllium 4											11 B Boron 5	12 C Carbon 6	14 N Nitrogen 7	16 O Oxygen 8	19 F Fluorine 9	20 Ne Neon 10
3	23 Na Sodium 11	24 Mg Magnesium 12											27 Al Aluminium 13	28 Si Silicon 14	31 P Phosphorus 15	32 S Sulphur 16	35.5 Cl Chlorine 17	40 Ar Argon 18
4	39 K Potassium 19	40 Ca Calcium 20	45 Sc Scandium 21	48 Ti Titanium 22	51 V Vanadium 23	52 Cr Chromium 24	55 Mn Manganese 25	56 Fe Iron 26	59 Co Cobalt 27	59 Ni Nickel 28	64 Cu Copper 29	65 Zn Zinc 30	70 Ga Gallium 31	73 Ge Germanium 32	75 As Arsenic 33	79 Se Selenium 34	80 Br Bromine 35	84 Kr Krypton 36
5	86 Rb Rubidium 37	88 Sr Strontium 38	89 Y Yttrium 39	91 Zr Zirconium 40	93 Nb Niobium 41	96 Mo Molybdenum 42	99 Tc Technetium 43	101 Ru Ruthenium 44	103 Rh Rhodium 45	106 Pd Palladium 46	108 Ag Silver 47	112 Cd Cadmium 48	115 In Indium 49	119 Sn Tin 50	122 Sb Antimony 51	128 Te Tellurium 52	127 I Iodine 53	131 Xe Xenon 54
6	133 Cs Caesium 55	137 Ba Barium 56	57-71 Lanthanides	179 Hf Hafnium 72	181 Ta Tantalum 73	184 W Tungsten 74	186 Re Rhenium 75	190 Os Osmium 76	192 Ir Iridium 77	195 Pt Platinum 78	197 Au Gold 79	201 Hg Mercury 80	204 Tl Thallium 81	207 Pb Lead 82	209 Bi Bismuth 83	210 Po Polonium 84	210 At Astatine 85	222 Rn Radon 86
7	223 Fr Francium 87	226 Ra Radium 88	89-103 Actinides															

mass number ➤ 4
proton number ➤ 2
He Helium

reactive metals — transition elements — poor metals — non metals — noble gases — separates metals from non-metals

The Periodic Table is Ace

1) The modern Periodic Table shows the elements in order of _proton number_.
2) The Periodic Table is laid out so that elements with _similar properties_ form in _columns_.
3) These _vertical columns_ are called _Groups_ and Roman Numerals are often used for them.
4) For example the _Group II_ elements are Be, Mg, Ca, Sr, Ba and Ra.
   They're all _metals_ which form 2+ ions and they have many other similar properties.
5) The _rows_ are called _periods_. Each new period represents another _full shell_ of electrons.

The Elements of a _Group_ Have the Same _Outer Electrons_

1) The elements in each _Group_ all have the same number of _electrons_ in their _outer shell_.
2) That's why they have _similar properties_. And that's why we arrange them in this way.
3) You absolutely must get that into your head if you want to _understand_ any Chemistry.

   The properties of the elements are decided _entirely_ by how many electrons they have.
   Proton number is therefore very significant because it is equal to how many electrons each atom has.
   But it's the number of electrons in the _outer shell_ which is the really important thing.

Electron Shells are just Totally Brill

The fact that electrons form shells around atoms is the reason for the whole of chemistry.
If they just whizzed round the nucleus any old how and didn't care about shells or any of that stuff there'd be no chemical reactions. No nothing in fact — because nothing would happen.
Without shells there'd be no atoms wanting to gain, lose or share electrons to form full shell arrangements. So they wouldn't be interested in forming ions or covalent bonds. Nothing would bother and nothing would happen. The atoms would just slob about, all day long. Just like teenagers.
But amazingly, they _do_ form shells (if they didn't, we wouldn't even be here to wonder about it), and the electron arrangement of each atom determines the whole of its chemical behaviour.
Phew. I mean electron arrangements explain practically the whole Universe. They're just totally brill.

Electron Shells — where would we be without them...

Make sure you learn the whole periodic table including every name, symbol and number.
No, only kidding! Just _learn_ the numbered points and _scribble_ them down, _mini-essay style_.

Electron Arrangements

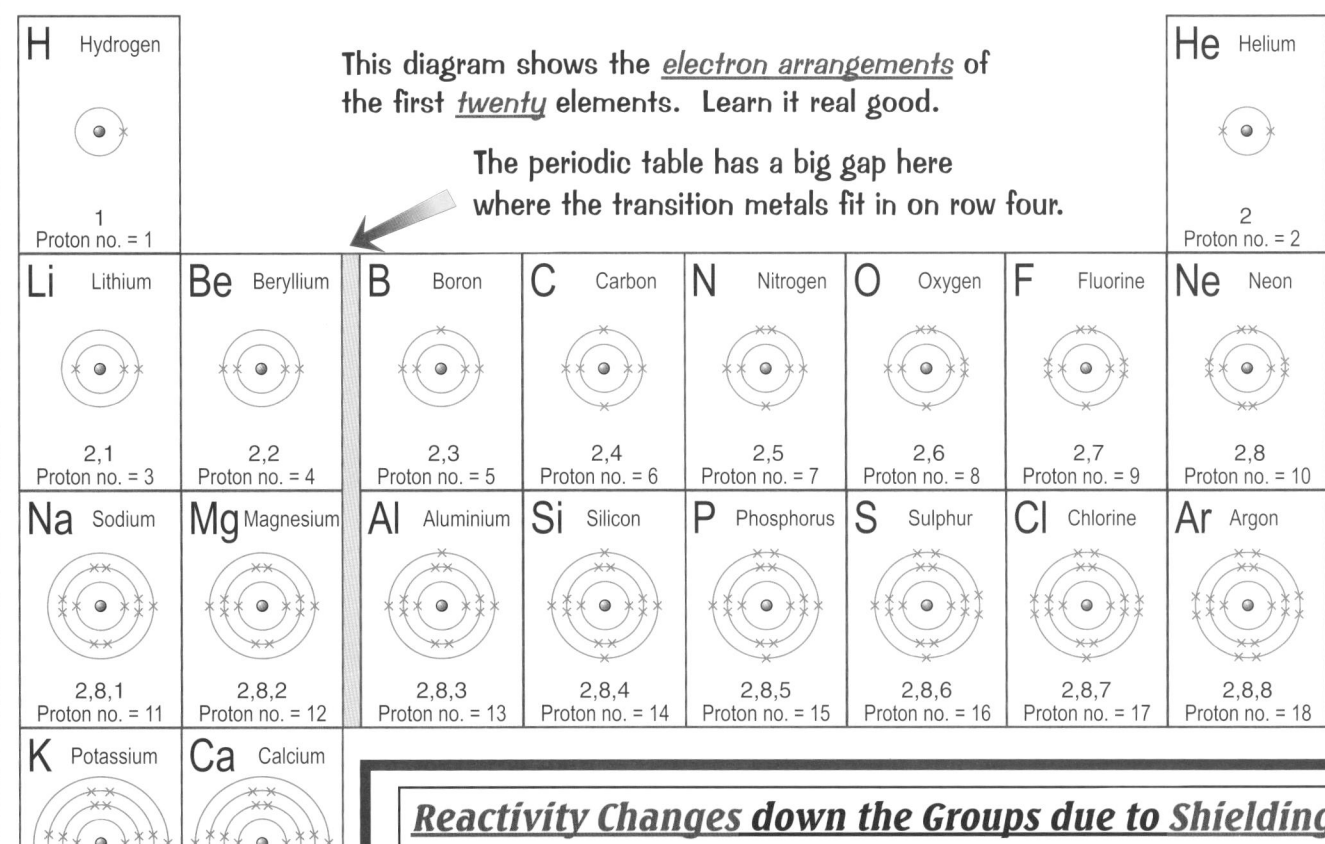

This diagram shows the *electron arrangements* of the first *twenty* elements. Learn it real good.

The periodic table has a big gap here where the transition metals fit in on row four.

Reactivity Changes *down* the Groups due to *Shielding*

1) As Atoms get *bigger*, they have more *full shells* of electrons.
2) As you go down any Group, each *new row* has *one more* full shell.
3) The number of *outer* electrons is the *same* for each element in a Group.
4) However the outer shell of electrons is *increasingly far* from the nucleus.
5) You have to learn to say that the inner shells provide *'SHIELDING'*.
6) This means that the *outer shell* electrons get *shielded* from the *attraction* of the *+ve nucleus*. The upshot of all this is:

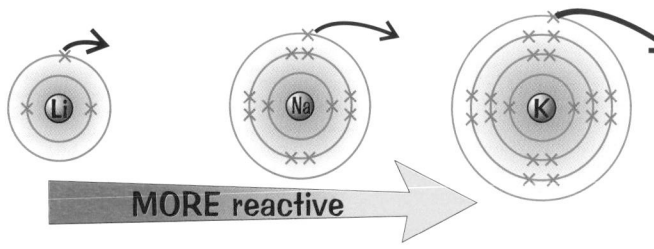

MORE reactive

As metal atoms get bigger, the outer electron is more easily lost.

This makes **METALS MORE REACTIVE** as you go **DOWN** Group I and Group II

As non-metal atoms get bigger, the extra electrons are harder to gain.

This makes **NON-METALS LESS REACTIVE** as you go **DOWN** Group VI and Group VII

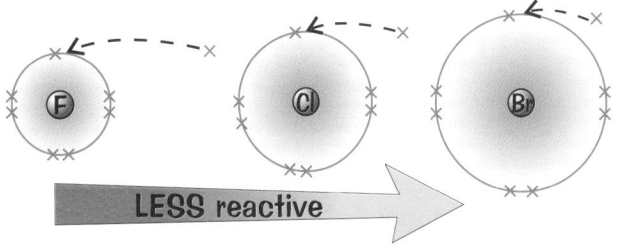

LESS reactive

Higher Higher Higher (left margin)

Higher Higher Higher (right margin)

Learn about Electron Shielding — and keep up with the trends...

Really, you should know enough about electron shells already to do that whole diagram at the top of the page without looking at it. Obviously you don't learn every atom separately — you learn the pattern. Also learn about the trends in reactivity. *Then cover the page and see what you know — by scribbling.*

Group O — The Noble Gases

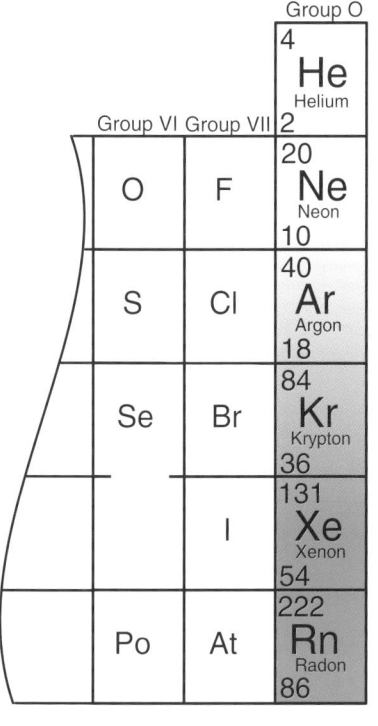

Group O

	Group VI	Group VII	
			4 **He** Helium 2
	O	F	20 **Ne** Neon 10
	S	Cl	40 **Ar** Argon 18
	Se	Br	84 **Kr** Krypton 36
		I	131 **Xe** Xenon 54
	Po	At	222 **Rn** Radon 86

As you go down the Group:

1) The density increases

because the atomic mass increases.

2) The boiling point increases

Helium boils at –269°C (that's cold!)
Xenon boils at –108°C (that's still cold)

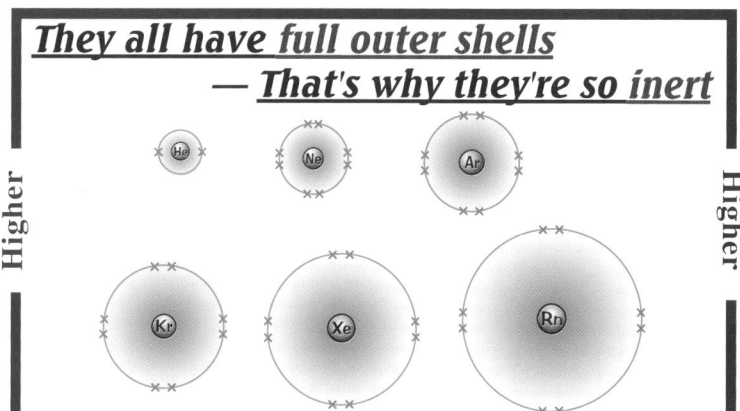

They all have full outer shells
— That's why they're so inert

Higher / Higher

HELIUM, NEON AND ARGON ARE NOBLE GASES

There's also _Krypton_, _Xenon_ and _Radon_, which may get asked.
They're also sometimes called the _Inert_ gases. Inert means "doesn't react".

THEY'RE ALL COLOURLESS, MONATOMIC GASES

Most gases are made up of _molecules_, but these _only exist_ as
individual atoms, because they _won't form bonds_ with anything.

Any noble gas

Neon! Fancy a bit of...bonding?

Neon! Forget it pal!

THE NOBLE GASES DON'T REACT AT ALL

Helium, Neon and Argon don't form _any kind of chemical bonds_ with anything.
They _always_ exist as separate atoms. They won't even join up in pairs.

HELIUM IS USED IN AIRSHIPS AND PARTY BALLOONS

Helium is ideal: it has very _low density_ and _won't
set on fire_, (like hydrogen does!)

Helium is ace!

I love Helium

And safe too!

NEON IS USED IN ELECTRICAL DISCHARGE TUBES

When a current is passed through neon it gives out a bright light.

neon is ace

ARGON IS USED IN FILAMENT LAMPS (LIGHT BULBS)

It provides an _inert atmosphere_ which stops the very hot
filament from _burning away_.

All these bulbs, argon

Eh? They look O.K. to me

ALL THREE ARE USED IN LASERS TOO

There's the famous little red _Helium-Neon_ laser
and the more powerful _Argon_ laser.

He-Ne laser   O - oh   Argon laser

They don't react — that's Noble De-use to us Chemists...

Well they don't react so there's obviously not much to learn about these. Nevertheless, there's
likely to be several questions on them so _make sure you learn everything on this page_.

Group I — The Alkali Metals

Learn These Trends:

As you go _DOWN_ Group I,
the Alkali Metals become:

1) Bigger atoms
...because there's one extra full shell of electrons for each row you go down.

2) More Reactive
...because the outer electron is more easily lost, because it's further from the nucleus.

3) Higher density
because the atoms have more mass.

4) Even Softer to cut

5) Lower melting point

6) Lower boiling point

Group I	Group II
7 **Li** Lithium 3	Be
23 **Na** Sodium 11	Mg
39 **K** Potassium 19	Ca
85.5 **Rb** Rubidium 37	Sr
133 **Cs** Caesium 55	Ba
223 **Fr** Francium 87	Ra

These _Group II_ metals are quite similar to Group I, except that they have two electrons in the outer shell and form 2+ ions.
They are less reactive.

1) The Alkali metals are very Reactive
They have to be _stored in oil_ and handled with _forceps_ (they burn the skin).

2) They are: Lithium, Sodium, Potassium and a couple more
Know those three names real well. They may also mention Rubidium and Caesium.

3) The Alkali Metals all have ONE outer electron
This makes them very _reactive_ and gives them all similar properties.

4) The Alkali Metals all form 1$^+$ ions
They are _keen to lose_ their one outer electron to from a _1$^+$ ion_:

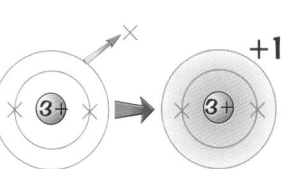

5) The Alkali metals always form Ionic Compounds
They are so keen to lose the outer electron there's _no way_ they'd consider _sharing_, so covalent bonding is _out of the question_.

6) The Alkali metals are soft — they cut with a knife
Lithium is the hardest, but still easy to cut with a scalpel.
They're _shiny_ when freshly cut, but _soon go dull_ as they react with the air.

7) The Alkali metals melt and boil easily (for metals)
Lithium melts at 180°C, Caesium at 29°C. Lithium boils at 1330°C, Caesium at 670°C.

8) The Alkali metals have low density (they float)
Lithium, Sodium and Potassium are all _less dense than water_. The others _"float"_ anyway, on H_2.

Learn about Alkali Metals — or get your fingers burnt...
Phew, now we're getting into the seriously dreary facts section. This takes a bit of learning this stuff does, especially those trends in behaviour as you go down the group. _Enjoy_.

Reactions of the Alkali Metals

Reaction with Cold Water produces Hydrogen Gas

Squeaky pop!!

H₂ H₂ H₂

fizz fizz

fizz fizz

The solution becomes *alkaline*, which changes the colour of the pH indicator to *purple*.

1) When *lithium*, *sodium* or *potassium* are put in *water*, they react very *vigorously*.
2) They *move* around the surface, *fizzing* furiously.
3) They produce *hydrogen*.   Potassium gets hot enough to *ignite* it.
4) A lighted splint will *indicate* hydrogen by producing the notorious '*squeaky pop*' as the H_2 ignites.
5) Sodium and potassium *melt* in the heat of the reaction.
6) They form a *hydroxide* in solution.
7) This will make universal indicator change from *green* to *purple*.

$$2Li_{(s)} + 2H_2O_{(l)} \rightarrow 2LiOH_{(aq)} + H_{2\,(g)}$$
$$2Na_{(s)} + 2H_2O_{(l)} \rightarrow 2NaOH_{(aq)} + H_{2\,(g)}$$
$$2K_{(s)} + 2H_2O_{(l)} \rightarrow 2KOH_{(aq)} + H_{2\,(g)}$$

Reaction with Chlorine etc. to produce Neutral Salts

Lithium, *sodium* and *potassium* all react *very vigorously* with *chlorine* when *heated*. They produce *chloride salts*.

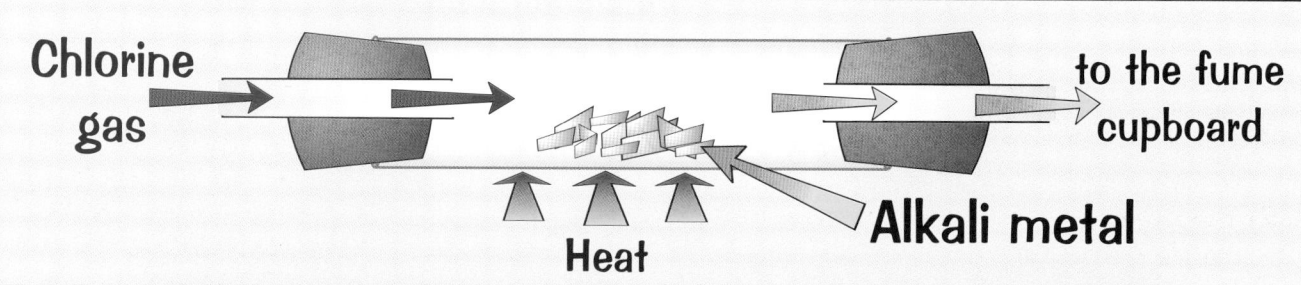

Chlorine gas

to the fume cupboard

Alkali metal

Heat

Learn these easy equations:

$$2Li_{(s)} + Cl_{2\,(g)} \rightarrow 2LiCl_{(s)} \text{ (lithium chloride)}$$
$$2Na_{(s)} + Cl_{2\,(g)} \rightarrow 2NaCl_{(s)} \text{ (sodium chloride)}$$
$$2K_{(s)} + Cl_{2\,(g)} \rightarrow 2KCl_{(s)} \text{ (potassium chloride)}$$

Fluorine, *bromine* and *iodine* produce similar salts such as *lithium fluoride* or *potassium bromide* or *sodium iodide* etc. etc.   All these *alkali metal salts* will cheerfully *dissolve* in water.

Reactions of the Alkali Metals

Periodic Table

Alkali Metals *burn in Air* to produce *Oxides*

All the alkali metals *burn in air* and in the process turn into oxides.
You ought to be able to repeat these easy equations with no more effort than a mere flick of the pencil:

$$4Li_{(s)} + O_{2(g)} \rightarrow 2Li_2O_{(s)} \text{ (lithium oxide)}$$
$$4Na_{(s)} + O_{2(g)} \rightarrow 2Na_2O_{(s)} \text{ (sodium oxide)}$$
$$4K_{(s)} + O_{2(g)} \rightarrow 2K_2O_{(s)} \text{ (potassium oxide)}$$

They all *burn in air* with *pretty coloured flames*:

Lithium burns with a *Bright red* flame:

Sodium burns with a *Bright orange* flame:

Potassium burns with a *Bright lilac* flame:

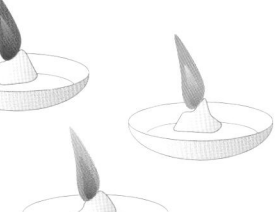

Alkali Metal *Oxides* and *Hydroxides* are *Alkaline*

This means that they'll react with *acids* to form *neutral salts*, like this:

$$NaOH + HCl \rightarrow H_2O + NaCl \text{ (a salt)}$$
$$Na_2O + 2HCl \rightarrow H_2O + 2NaCl \text{ (a salt)}$$
$$KOH + HCl \rightarrow H_2O + KCl \text{ (a salt)}$$
$$K_2O + 2HCl \rightarrow H_2O + 2KCl \text{ (a salt)}$$

All Alkali Metal Compounds look like "Salt" and Dissolve with Glee

1) All alkali metal compounds are *ionic*, so they form *crystals* which *dissolve* easily.

2) They're all very *stable* because the alkali metals are so *reactive*.

3) And because they always form *ionic* compounds with *giant ionic structures*, the compounds *all* look pretty much like the regular *"salt"* you put in your chip butties.

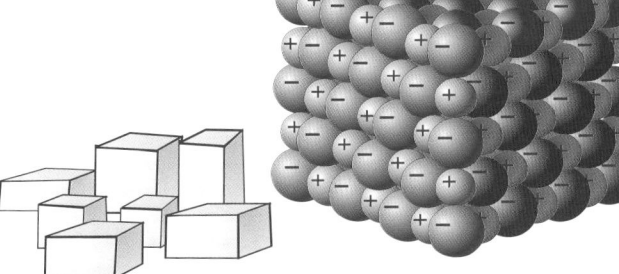

The Notorious Squeaky Pop? — weren't they a Rock Band...

This stuff's pretty grisly isn't it. Still, if you keep covering the page and repeating bits back to yourself, or scribbling bits down, then little by little *it does go in*. Little by little. *Nicely*.

58

Group VII — The Halogens

Periodic Table

Learn These Trends:

As you go _DOWN_ Group VII, the _HALOGENS_ become:

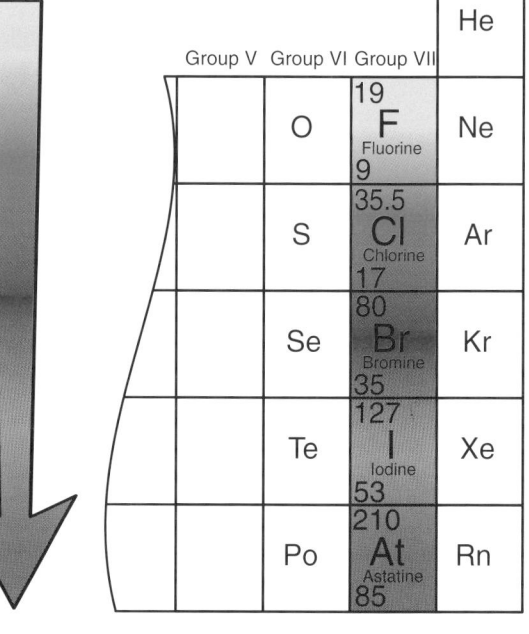

1) Bigger atoms
...because there's one extra full shell of electrons for each row you go down.

2) Less Reactive
...because there's less inclination to gain the extra electron to fill the outer shell when it's further out from the nucleus.

3) Darker in colour

4) They go from gas to solid
Fluorine and _chlorine_ are _gases_, _bromine_ is a _liquid_, and _iodine_ is a _solid_.

5) Higher melting point

6) Higher boiling point

---

1) The Halogens are all non-metals with coloured vapours

Fluorine is a very reactive, poisonous _yellow gas_.
Chlorine is a fairly reactive poisonous _dense green gas_.
Bromine is a dense, poisonous, _red-brown volatile liquid_.
Iodine is a _dark grey_ crystalline _solid_ or a _purple vapour_.

---

2) They all form molecules which are pairs of atoms:

F_2  Cl_2 Br_2 I_2

---

3) The Halogens do both ionic and covalent bonding

The Halogens all form _ions with a 1⁻ charge_: F^- Cl^- Br^- I^- as in Na^+Cl^- or $Fe^{3+}Br^-_3$
They form _covalent bonds_ with _themselves_ and in various _molecular compounds_ like these:

Carbon tetrachloride:
(CCl₄)

Hydrogen chloride:
(HCl)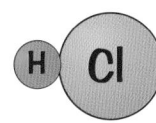

---

4) The Halogens are poisonous — always use a fume cupboard

What else can I say? Use a fume cupboard, or else...

I've never liked Halogens — they give me a bad head...

Well, I think Halogens are just slightly less grim than the Alkali metals. At least they change colour and go from gases to liquid to solid. _Learn the boring facts anyway_. And smile ☺.

Reactions of The Halogens

1) The Halogens react with metals to form salts

They react with most metals including *iron* and *aluminium*, to form *salts* (or *'metal halides'*).

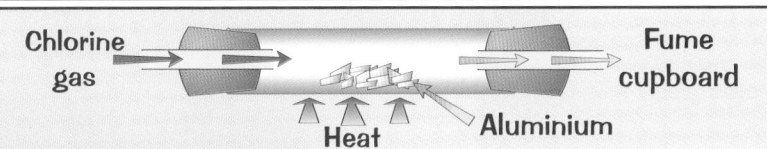

Chlorine gas — Heat — Aluminium — Fume cupboard

Equations:

$$2Al_{(s)} + 3Cl_{2(g)} \rightarrow 2AlCl_{3(s)} \text{ (Aluminium chloride)}$$

$$2Fe_{(s)} + 3Br_{2(g)} \rightarrow 2FeBr_{3(s)} \text{ (Iron(III) bromide)}$$

Chloride, Bromide and Iodide salts are sorted using Silver Nitrate

Metal halide salts like the ones above are *ionic* so they usually *dissolve*.
However, the *SILVER* halide salts are *not* soluble and this gives a good *test* for the *three* halides:

1) Adding *silver nitrate* to a *chloride* produces a *white* precipitate (of *silver chloride*).
2) Adding *silver nitrate* to a *bromide* produces a *creamy-coloured* precipitate (of *silver bromide*).
3) Adding *silver nitrate* to an *iodide* produces a *yellow* precipitate (of *silver iodide*).

2) More reactive Halogens will displace less reactive ones

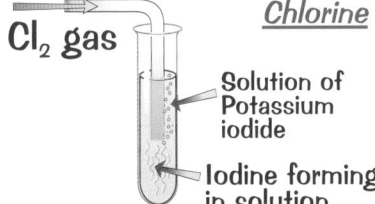

Cl_2 gas

Solution of Potassium iodide

Iodine forming in solution

Chlorine can displace *bromine* and *iodine* from a solution of *bromide* or *iodide*.
Bromine will also displace *iodine* because of the *trend* in *reactivity*.

$$Cl_{2(g)} + 2KI_{(aq)} \rightarrow I_{2(aq)} + 2KCl_{(aq)}$$
$$Cl_{2(g)} + 2KBr_{(aq)} \rightarrow Br_{2(aq)} + 2KCl_{(aq)}$$

3) Hydrogen Chloride gas dissolves to form HCl acid

1) *Hydrogen chloride* is a *diatomic* molecule, (a two atom molecule) held together by a *covalent* bond.
2) It has a *simple molecular* structure.
3) It is a *dense, colourless gas* with a choking smell.
4) Gaseous hydrogen chloride is important in the manufacture of *polymers*.
5) It *dissolves* in water, which is very unusual for a covalent substance, to form the well-known strong acid, *hydrochloric acid*.
6) The *proper* method for dissolving hydrogen chloride in water is to use an *inverted funnel* as shown:
7) HCl gas *reacts with water* to produce H^+ *ions*, which is what

makes it *acidic*:

$$HCl_{(g)} \xrightarrow{water} H^+_{(aq)} + Cl^-_{(aq)}$$

Hydrogen Chloride — Cl H — Covalent bond

Hydrogen Chloride

Hydrogen Bromide and Hydrogen Iodide do the same

Just like hydrogen chloride, these two *gases* will also *dissolve easily* to form *strong acids*:

$$HBr_{(g)} \rightarrow H^+_{(aq)} + Br^-_{(aq)}$$
$$HI_{(g)} \rightarrow H^+_{(aq)} + I^-_{(aq)}$$

Salts and Acids — what an unsavoury combination...

More exciting reactions to delight and entertain you through the shove and shuffle of your otherwise dreary teenage years. Think of all the poor third-world children who never get to learn about chloride salts and hydrogen bromide — you're very lucky. *Learn and enjoy...*

Transition Metals

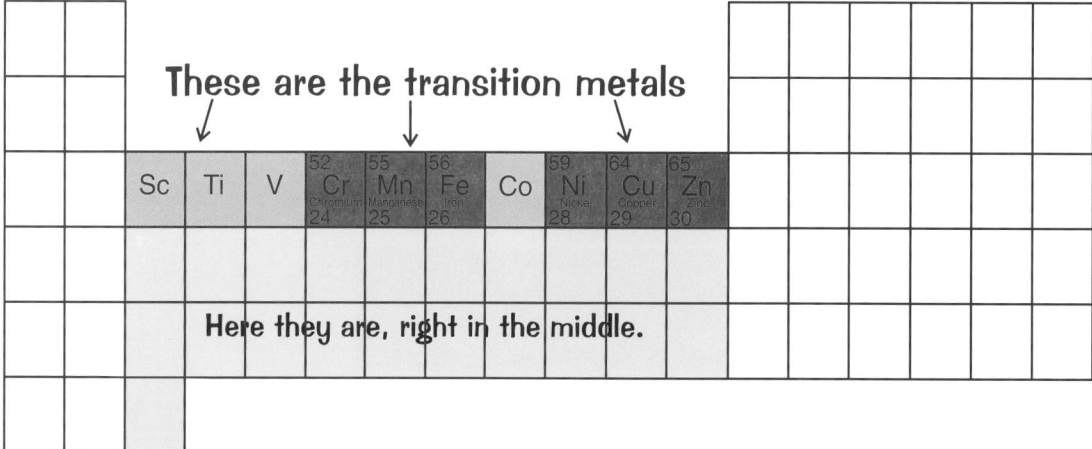

These are the transition metals

| | | | 52 Cr Chromium 24 | 55 Mn Manganese 25 | 56 Fe Iron 26 | | 59 Ni Nickel 28 | 64 Cu Copper 29 | 65 Zn Zinc 30 |
| Sc | Ti | V | | | | Co | | | |

Here they are, right in the middle.

Chromium, Manganese, Iron, Nickel, Copper, Zinc

You need to know the ones shown in red fairly well. If they wanted to be mean in the Exam *(if!)* they could cheerfully mention one of the others like scandium or cobalt or titanium or vanadium. Don't let it hassle you. They'll just be testing how well you can *"apply scientific knowledge to new information"*. In other words, just assume these "new" transition metals follow all the properties you've already learnt for the others. That's all it is, but it can really worry some folk.

Transition Metals *all have* high melting point *and* high density

They're *typical* metals. They have the properties you would expect of a proper metal:
1) *Good conductors* of heat and electricity.
2) Very *dense*, *strong* and *shiny*.
3) Iron melts at 1500°C, copper melts at 1100°C and zinc melts at 400°C.

Transition Metals *and their* compounds *all make good catalysts*

1) *Iron* is the catalyst used in the *Haber process* for making *ammonia*.
2) *Manganese (IV) oxide* is a good catalyst for the decomposition of *hydrogen peroxide*.
3) *Nickel* is useful for turning *oils into fats* for making margarine.

The compounds *are very colourful*

1) The compounds are colourful due to the *transition metal ion* which they contain.   e.g. Potassium chromate (VI) is *yellow*.
        Potassium manganate(VII) is *purple*.
        Copper (II) sulphate is *blue*.
2) The colour of people's *hair* and also the colours in *gemstones* like *blue sapphires* and *green emeralds* are all due to *transition metals*.

Transition metals produce many useful alloys

1) The transition metals can be easily *mixed* (when molten) to produce a *new* metal with different properties to the original metals. The new metal is called an *alloy*.
2) For example, the transition metals *zinc* and *copper* make the alloy *brass* for trumpets and tubas.

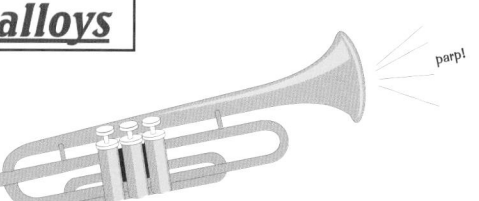
parp!

Lots of pretty colours — that's what we like to see...

There's quite a few things to learn about transition metals. First try to remember the three headings. Then learn the details that go under each one. *Keep trying to scribble it all down.*

Acids and Alkalis

The pH Scale and Universal Indicator

pH 1 2 3 4 5 6 7 8 9 10 11 12 13 14

ACIDS   NEUTRAL   ALKALIS

car battery acid, stomach acid | vinegar, lemon juice | acid rain | normal rain | tap water, milk | washing up liquid | pancreatic juice | soap powder | ammonia

An Indicator is just a Dye that changes colour

The dye changes _colour_ depending on whether it's in an _acid_ or in an _alkali_.
Universal indicator is a very useful combination of dyes which give the colours shown above.

The pH scale goes from 1 to 14

1) The _strongest acid_ has _pH 1_.   The _strongest alkali_ has _pH 14_.
2) If something is _neutral_ it has _pH 7_ (e.g. pure water).
3) Anything less than 7 is _acid_. Anything more than 7 is _alkaline_. (An alkali can also be called a base.)

Acids have H⁺ ions   Alkalis have OH⁻ ions

The _strict definitions_ of acids and alkalis are:

ACIDS are substances which form $H^+_{(aq)}$ _ions_ when added to _water_.

ALKALIS are substances which form $OH^-_{(aq)}$ _ions_ when added to _water_.

Neutralisation

This is the equation for _any_ neutralisation reaction. Make sure you learn it:

Acid + alkali → salt + water

Neutralisation can also be seen _in terms of ions_ like this, so learn it too:

$$H^+_{(aq)} + OH^-_{(aq)} \rightarrow H_2O_{(l)}$$

Three "Real life" Examples of Neutralisation:

1) _Indigestion_ is caused by too much _hydrochloric acid_ in the stomach.
   Indigestion tablets contain _alkalis_ such as _magnesium oxide_, which _neutralise_ the excess HCl.

2) _Fields_ with _acidic soils_ can be improved no end by adding _lime_ (See P.28).
   The lime added to fields is _calcium hydroxide_ $Ca(OH)_2$ which is of course an _alkali_.

3) _Lakes_ affected by _acid rain_ can also be _neutralised_ by adding _lime_. This saves the fish.

Hey man, like "acid", yeah — eeuuucch...

Try and enjoy this page on acids and alkalis, because it gets _really_ tedious from now on. These are very basic facts and possibly quite interesting. _Cover the page and scribble them down._

Acids Reacting With Metals

Acid + Metal → Salt + Hydrogen

That's written big 'cos it's kinda worth remembering.   Here's the *typical experiment*:

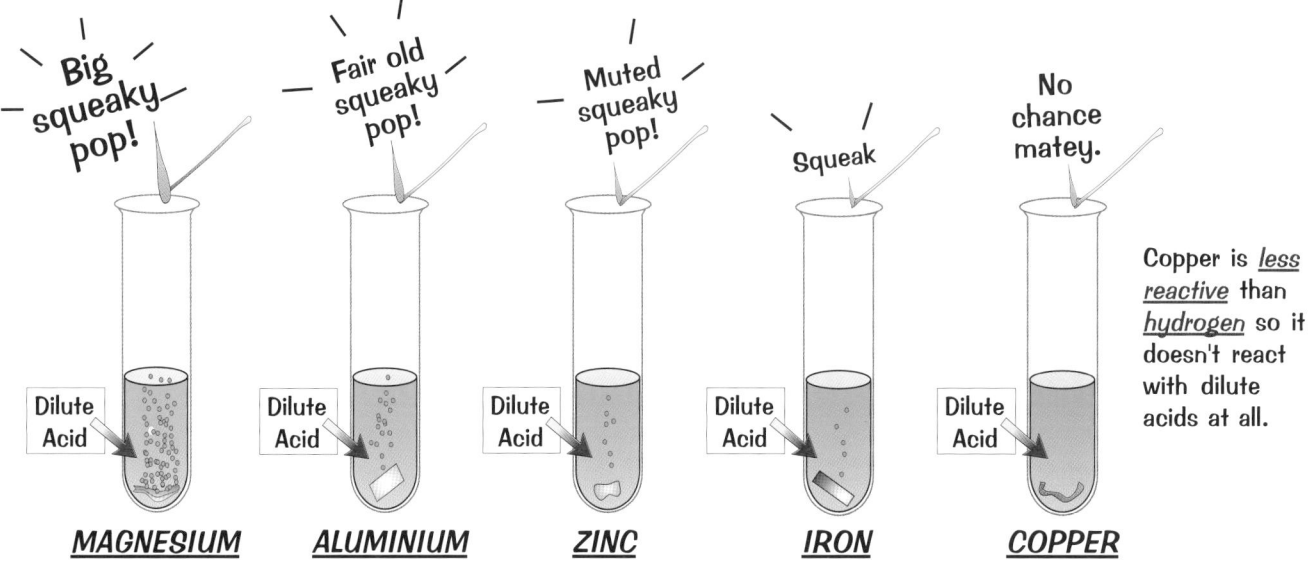

1) The more *reactive* the metal, the *faster* it will go.

2) *Copper* does *not* react with dilute acids *at all* — because it's *less* reactive than *hydrogen*.

3) The *speed* of reaction is indicated by the *rate* at which the *bubbles* of hydrogen are given off.

4) The *hydrogen* is confirmed by the *burning splint test* giving the notorious 'squeaky pop'.

5) The *type of salt* produced depends on which *metal* is used, and which *acid* is used:

Hydrochloric acid will always produce chloride salts:

$$2HCl + Mg \rightarrow MgCl_2 + H_2$$ (Magnesium chloride)

$$6HCl + 2Al \rightarrow 2AlCl_3 + 3H_2$$ (Aluminium chloride)

$$2HCl + Zn \rightarrow ZnCl_2 + H_2$$ (Zinc chloride)

Sulphuric acid will always produce sulphate salts:

$$H_2SO_4 + Mg \rightarrow MgSO_4 + H_2$$ (Magnesium sulphate)

$$3H_2SO_4 + 2Al \rightarrow Al_2(SO_4)_3 + 3H_2$$ (Aluminium sulphate)

$$H_2SO_4 + Zn \rightarrow ZnSO_4 + H_2$$ (Zinc sulphate)

Nitric acid produces nitrate salts when NEUTRALISED, but...

Nitric acid reacts fine with alkalis, to produce nitrates, but it can play silly devils with metals and produce nitrogen oxides instead, so we'll ignore it here. Chemistry's a real messy subject sometimes, innit.

Revision of Acids and Metals — easy as squeaky pop...

Actually, this stuff isn't too bad I don't think. I mean it's *fairly* interesting. Not quite in the same league as The Spice Girls, I grant you, but for Chemistry it's not bad at all. At least there's bubbles and flames and noise and that kinda thing. Anyway, *learn it, scribble it down, etc...*

Acids with Oxides and Hydroxides

Metal Oxides and Metal Hydroxides are Alkalis

1) Some *metal oxides* and *metal hydroxides* dissolve in *water* to produce *alkaline* solutions.
2) In other words, metal oxides and metal hydroxides are generally *alkalis*.
3) This means they'll react with *acids* to form a *salt* and *water*.
4) Even those that won't dissolve in water will still react with acid.

Acid + Metal Oxide → Salt + Water

Acid + Metal Hydroxide → Salt + Water

(These are *neutralisation reactions* of course)

The Combination of Metal and Acid decides the Salt

This isn't exactly exciting but it's pretty easy, so try and get the hang of it:

Hydrochloric acid	+	Copper oxide	→	Copper chloride	+ water
Hydrochloric acid	+	Sodium hydroxide	→	Sodium chloride	+ water
Sulphuric acid	+	Zinc oxide	→	Zinc sulphate	+ water
Sulphuric acid	+	Calcium hydroxide	→	Calcium sulphate	+ water
Nitric acid	+	Magnesium oxide	→	Magnesium nitrate	+ water
Nitric acid	+	Potassium hydroxide	→	Potassium nitrate	+ water

The symbol equations are all pretty much the same. Here's two of them:

$$H_2SO_4 + ZnO \rightarrow ZnSO_4 + H_2O$$
$$HNO_3 + KOH \rightarrow KNO_3 + H_2O$$

The Oxides of non-metals are usually acidic, not alkaline

1) The best examples are the *oxides* of these three non-metals: *carbon*, *sulphur* and *nitrogen*.
2) *Carbon dioxide* dissolves in water to form *carbonic acid* which is a *weak* acid.
3) *Sulphur Dioxide* combines with water and O_2 to form *sulphuric acid* which is a *strong* acid.
4) *Nitrogen dioxide* dissolves in water to form *nitric acid* which is a *strong* acid.
5) These three are all present in *acid rain* of course.
6) The *carbonic acid* is present in rain anyway, so even *ordinary* rain is slightly acidic.
   Remember the three examples:

Non-metal oxides are acidic:
Carbon dioxide   Sulphur dioxide   Nitrogen dioxide

Acids are really dull, aren't they — learn and snore...

You've gotta be a pretty serious career chemist to find this stuff interesting.
Normal people (like you and me!) just have to grin and bear it. Oh, and *learn it* as well, of course
— don't forget the small matter of those little Exams you've got coming up... remember?

The Reactivity Series of Metals

You must learn this Reactivity Series

You really should know which are the more reactive metals and which are the less reactive ones.

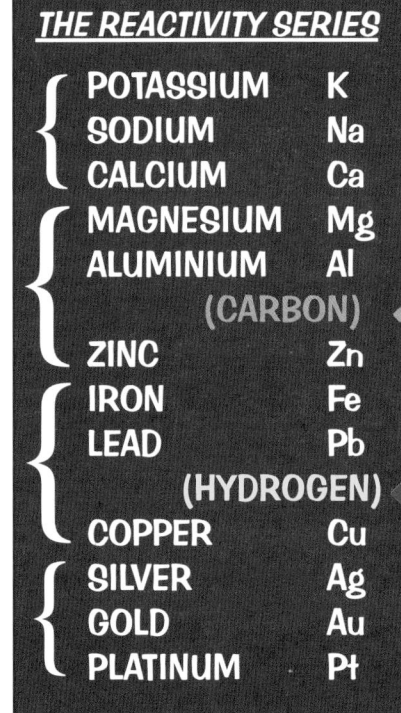

THE REACTIVITY SERIES

Very Reactive
POTASSIUM	K
SODIUM	Na
CALCIUM	Ca

Fairly Reactive
MAGNESIUM	Mg
ALUMINIUM	Al
(CARBON)	

Not very Reactive
ZINC	Zn
IRON	Fe
LEAD	Pb
(HYDROGEN)	
COPPER	Cu

Not at all Reactive
SILVER	Ag
GOLD	Au
PLATINUM	Pt

Metals *above carbon* must be extracted from their ores by *electrolysis*.

Metals *below carbon* can be extracted from their ore using *reduction* with *coke or charcoal*.

Metals *below hydrogen* don't react with *water* or *acid*. They don't easily *tarnish* or *corrode*.

This *reactivity series* was determined by doing experiments to see how *strongly* metals *react*. The *three standard reactions* to determine reactivity are with 1) *air* 2) *water* and 3) *dilute acid*. These are *important* so make sure you know about all three in reasonable detail, as follows:

Reacting Metals in Air

1) *Most metals* will lose their *bright surface* over a period of time (they "tarnish").
2) The *dull* finish they get is due to a layer of *oxide* that forms.
3) *Heating them* makes it easier to see how *reactive* they are, compared to each other.

layer of oxide

4) The equation is *real simple*:

Metal + Oxygen → Metal Oxide

Reaction with Air

POTASSIUM
SODIUM
CALCIUM
MAGNESIUM
} Burn very easily with a bright flame

ALUMINIUM
ZINC
IRON
LEAD
COPPER
} React slowly with air when heated

SILVER
GOLD
} No reaction

Examples: 1) $2Fe + O_2 \rightarrow 2FeO$ 2) $4Na + O_2 \rightarrow 2Na_2O$

How to get a good reaction — just smile ... ☺

Believe it or not they could easily give you a question asking what happens when copper is heated in air, and when calcium is heated in air. That means *all these details need learning*.

Reactivity of Metals

Reacting Metals With Water

1) If a *metal* reacts with *water* it will always release *hydrogen*.
2) The *more reactive* metals react with *cold water* to form *hydroxides*:

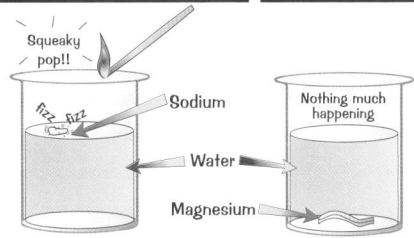

SODIUM + WATER → SODIUM HYDROXIDE + HYDROGEN

$$2Na + 2H_2O \rightarrow 2NaOH + H_2$$

3) The *less reactive* metals don't react quickly with water but *will* react with *steam* to form *oxides*:

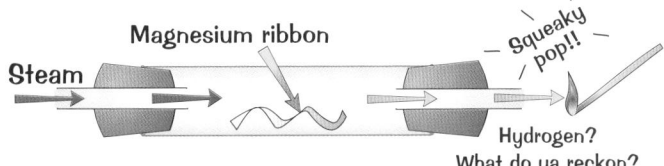

Magnesium ribbon
Steam
Squeaky pop!!
Hydrogen? What do ya reckon?

ZINC + WATER → ZINC OXIDE + HYDROGEN

$$Zn + H_2O \rightarrow ZnO + H_2$$

Reaction with Water

POTASSIUM SODIUM CALCIUM	React with cold water
MAGNESIUM ALUMINIUM ZINC	React with steam
IRON	Reacts reversibly with steam
LEAD COPPER SILVER GOLD	No reaction with water or steam

Reacting Metals With Dilute Acid

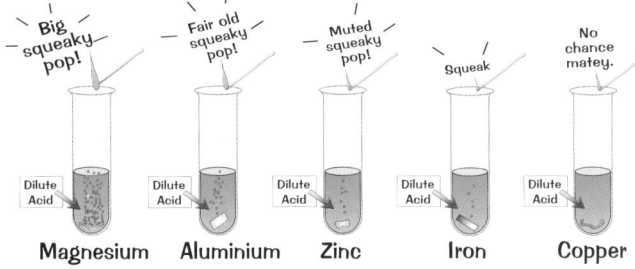

Big squeaky pop! — Magnesium
Fair old squeaky pop! — Aluminium
Muted squeaky pop! — Zinc
Squeak — Iron
No chance matey. — Copper

1) Metals *above* hydrogen in the reactivity series react with *acids*. Those *below* hydrogen *won't*.
2) The reaction becomes *slower* as you go *down the series* — as you'd *expect*.
3) The equation is real simple:

METAL + ACID → SALT + HYDROGEN

$$Mg + 2HCl \rightarrow MgCl_2 + H_2$$

Reaction with Dilute Acid

POTASSIUM SODIUM CALCIUM	Violent reaction with dilute acids
MAGNESIUM ALUMINIUM ZINC IRON	React fairly well with dilute acids
LEAD COPPER SILVER GOLD	No reaction with dilute acids

These reactions with water and acids are "Competition Reactions"

1) If the metal is *more reactive* than *hydrogen* it pushes the hydrogen *out*, hence the *bubbles*.
2) The metal *replaces* the hydrogen in the compound. E.g. in water, the metal "steals" the oxygen from the hydrogen to form a *metal oxide*. The *hydrogen* is then released as *gas bubbles*.
3) If the metal is *less reactive* than hydrogen, then it *won't* be able to displace it and *nothing will happen*.

All this just to say "some metals react more than others"...

I must say there's quite a lot of tricky details in these two pages. It's tempting to say that they can't possibly expect you to know them all. But then you look at the Exam questions and there they are, asking you precisely these kind of tricky details. Tough toffee, pal. *Learn and enjoy*.

Metal Displacement Reactions

There's only one *golden rule* here:

A *MORE* reactive metal will *displace* a *LESS* reactive metal from a compound

1) This is such a simple idea, surely.
2) You know all about the reactivity series — some metals react *more strongly* than *others*.
3) So if you put a *reactive* metal like magnesium in a chemical solution you'd expect it to react.
4) If the chemical solution is a *dissolved metal compound*, then the reactive metal that you add will *replace* the *less* reactive metal in the compound.
5) The metal that's *'kicked out'* will then appear as *fresh metal* somewhere in the solution.
6) But if the metal added is *less reactive* than the one in solution, then *no reaction* will take place.

The Virtually World Famous Iron Nail in Copper Sulphate demo

A *MORE* REACTIVE METAL WILL *DISPLACE* A *LESS* REACTIVE METAL:

1) Put an *iron* nail in a solution of *copper(II) sulphate* and you'll see *two* things happen:

   a) The iron nail will become coated with *copper*.
   b) The *blue* solution will turn *colourless*.

2) This is because the iron is *more* reactive than the copper and *displaces* it from the solution.
3) This produces *fresh copper metal* on the nail and a *colourless* solution of *iron sulphate*.

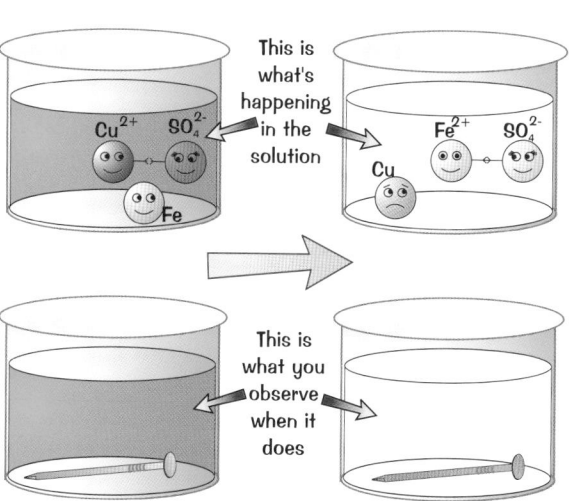

YOU'LL ALWAYS SEE A *DEPOSIT OF METAL* AND POSSIBLY A *COLOUR CHANGE*:

The equation is very very easy:

$$\text{iron} + \text{copper sulphate} \rightarrow \text{iron sulphate} + \text{copper}$$
$$\text{Fe} + \text{CuSO}_4 \rightarrow \text{FeSO}_4 + \text{Cu}$$

There are lots of different examples, but they're all the same...

Just remember the *golden rule* at the top of the page, and you can't go wrong.
The equations are always *simple*. The only tricky bit comes if the metals aren't both *2+ ions* like in this one:

$$\text{zinc} + \text{silver nitrate} \rightarrow \text{zinc nitrate} + \text{silver}$$
$$\text{Zn} + 2\text{AgNO}_3 \rightarrow \text{Zn(NO}_3)_2 + 2\text{Ag}$$

But remember, if the metal added is *less* reactive, nothing will happen.
For example if you add *iron* to *magnesium sulphate* there'll be *NO REACTION*.

Even atoms squabble — and I thought it was only school kids...

This is simple enough. Just make sure you learn all the little details. Then cover the page and scribble down a *mini-essay* of the main points. Then see what you missed. *Then try again*.

Corrosion of Metals

Reactive metals will form *oxides* quite quickly when exposed to the *air*.
Most metals form quite decent *hard oxides* that form a good *protective layer*.

But *iron*, woe of woes, does no such thing.
No, iron has to form the most appalling *red flaky oxide* imaginable — the metal we use the *most* just had to be the one that turns to horrible useless *rust*.
When God invented all the elements I bet he had a good old cackle to himself over that one.

The Rusting of Iron requires both Air and Water

The *classic experiment* on rust is to put *iron nails* in various test tubes to see *how quickly* they rust.

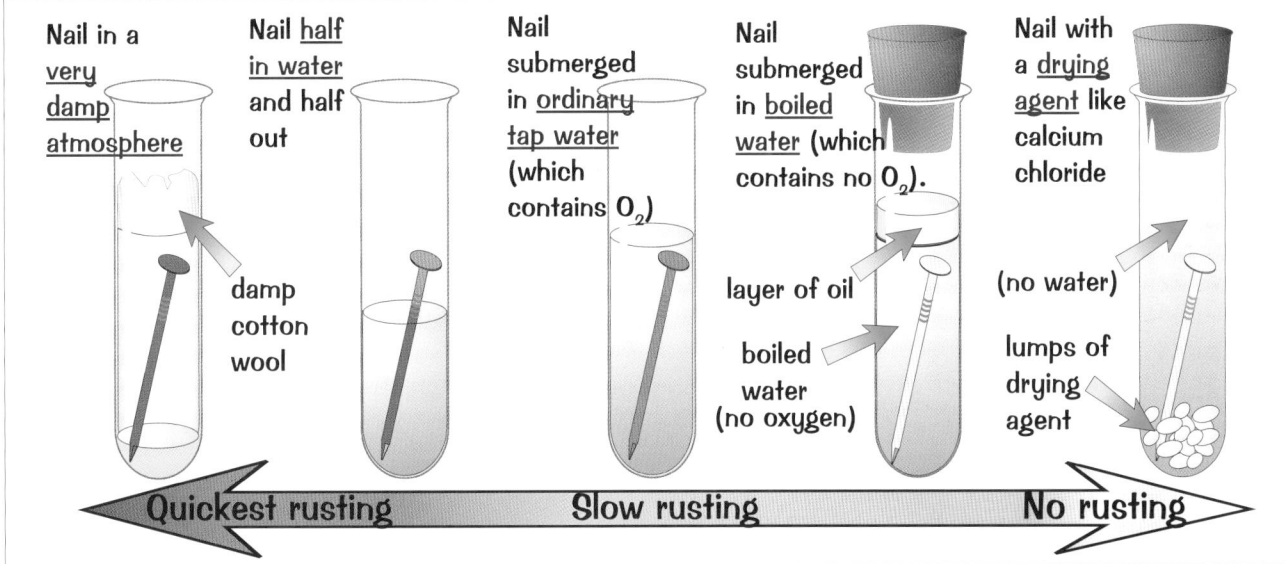

Nail in a *very damp atmosphere*

damp cotton wool

Nail *half in water* and half out

Nail submerged in *ordinary tap water* (which contains O_2)

Nail submerged in *boiled water* (which contains no O_2).

layer of oil

boiled water (no oxygen)

Nail with a *drying agent* like calcium chloride

(no water)

lumps of drying agent

Quickest rusting   Slow rusting   No rusting

The rusting is *quickest* where there is most *air and water* reaching the iron nail.
If *either* air or water is *totally absent* there'll be *no rusting at all*.

Rust is prevented by paint, oil or galvanising

1) *Painting* is OK but where the paint surface gets *damaged*, rust will get a grip and *spread*.

2) A coating of *oil or grease* is better on bits of *moving machinery* or on tools.
   However the oil has to be constantly re-applied because it soon wears or washes off.

Galvanising gives great protection even when damaged

1) *Galvanising* is the *best solution* to rust prevention but it's more expensive.
   Galvanising is a process that bonds a layer of *zinc metal* onto the surface of the *steel*.
   The zinc soon *reacts* with the air to form *zinc oxide* which gives a good *protective layer*.

2) The *big advantage* with galvanisation is that even if the zinc coating gets *scratched* or *damaged*, the exposed steel will *still* not rust!

Rust! Yeah, very funny, ho ho ho — but what about my little MGB...

At last! A page that has some relevance to everyday life. Who said you never learn anything useful at school. Not too much to learn here either. Try a couple of *mini-essays* and make sure you can draw all those pretty test tubes too. Then check back and see what you *missed*.

Metals

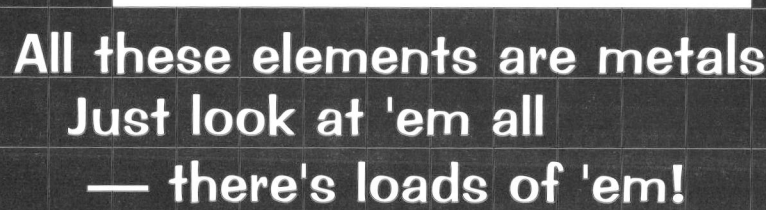

All these elements are metals
Just look at 'em all
— there's loads of 'em!

The Metallic Crystal Structure

1) All metals have the _same_ basic _properties_.
2) These are due to the _special type of bonding_ that exists in metals.
3) Metals consist of a _giant structure_ of atoms held together with _metallic bonds_.
4) These special bonds allow the _outer electron(s)_ of each atom to move _freely_.
5) This creates a '_sea_' of _free electrons_ throughout the metal which is what gives rise to many of the properties of metals.

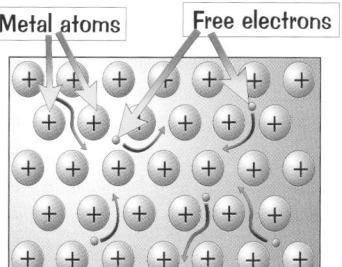

Metal atoms   Free electrons

1) They all conduct electricity

This is entirely due to the _free electrons_ which _carry_ the current.

2) They're all good conductors of heat

Again this is entirely due to the _free electrons_ which _carry the heat energy_ through the metal.

3) Metals are strong, but also bendy and malleable

They are _strong_ (hard to break), but they can be bent or hammered into a different shape.

Don't try this at home. You'll die.

4) They're all shiny (when freshly cut or polished)

5) They have high melting and boiling points

Which means you have to get them pretty _hot_ to _melt them_ (except good old mercury). e.g. copper 1100°C, tungsten 3377°C

6) They can be mixed together to form many useful alloys:

1) _Steel_ is an _alloy_ of _iron_ and about _1% carbon_. Steel is much less _brittle_ than iron.
2) _Bronze_ is an _alloy_ (mixture) of _copper and tin_. It's harder than copper but still easily shaped.
3) _Copper and nickel_ (75%:25%) are used to make _cupro-nickel_ which is hard enough for _coins_.

Metal Fatigue? — yeah, we've all had enough of this page now...

Phew.

Non-Metals

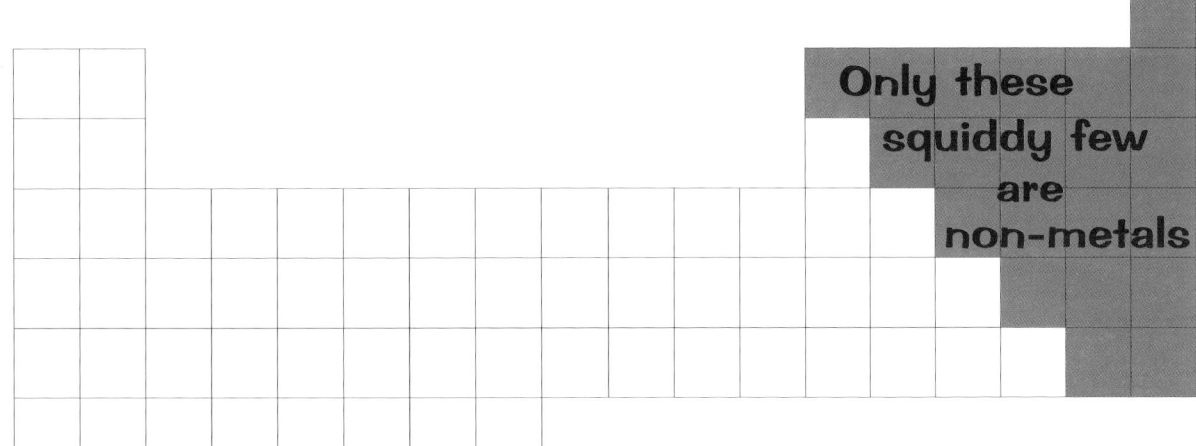

Non-Metal elements are either dull, brittle solids or they're gases

Only about a _quarter_ of the elements are _non-metals_.
Half the non-metals are _gases_ and half are _solids_.
Bromine is the only _liquid non-metal element_.
(Mercury is the only other element which is liquid — at _room temperature_, that is)

1) Non-metals are poor conductors of heat

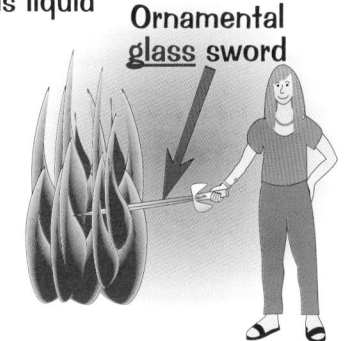

Ornamental glass sword

2) Non-metals don't conduct electricity at all

— except for _graphite_ which conducts because of it has some _free electrons_ between the _layers_ of its crystal structure.

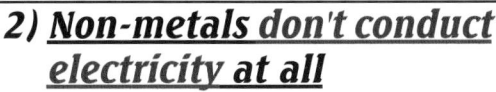

Ornamental glass sword

Don't try this either. Never mind why – just don't.

3) Non-metals usually bond in small molecules, e.g. O_2 N_2 etc.

4) But silicon and carbon form giant structures:

Graphite (pure carbon)

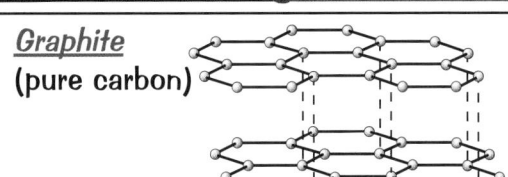

Diamond (pure carbon)

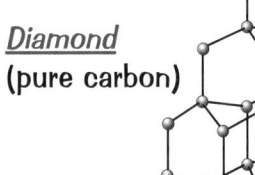

Non-metal Fatigue — I've just invented it, zzzzzzzz....

Metals and non-metals are really the only things that make Chemistry difficult. If it wasn't for them, the whole subject would be much more straightforward. _Learn and enjoy._

Industrial Salt

Salt is taken from the sea — and from underneath Cheshire

1) In _hot_ countries they just pour _sea water_ into big flat open _tanks_ and let the _sun_ evaporate the water to leave salt. This is no good in cold countries because there isn't enough sunshine.

2) In _Britain_ (a cold country — as if you need reminding), salt is extracted from _underground deposits_ left _millions_ of years ago when _ancient seas_ evaporated.

3) There are massive deposits of this _ROCK SALT_ in _Cheshire_.

4) The salt is extracted either by _mining_ or else by _pumping water_ into the deposit, _dissolving_ the salt, and then pumping the salt water back to the surface.

5) Rock salt is a mixture of mainly _sand and salt_. It can be used in its raw state on _roads_, or the salt can be filtered out for more _refined uses_.

1) Salt (sodium chloride) is widely used in the food industry

Salt is added to most _processed foods_ to enhance the _flavour_.
It's now reckoned to be _unhealthy_ to eat too much salt.
So just think about that next time you pour it on your chips.

> _I'm just waiting for the great day of reckoning when finally every single food has been declared either generally unhealthy or else downright dangerous. Perhaps we should all lay bets on what'll be the last food still considered safe to eat. My money's already on Spam Butties._

2) Rock salt is used for de-icing roads

1) The _salt_ in the mixture _melts ice_ by lowering the _freezing point_ of water to around -5°C.

2) The _sand and grit_ in it gives useful _grip_ on ice which hasn't melted.

3) Coincidentally, salt _speeds up_ the _corrosion_ process, making cars rust to bits in no time.

3) Salt is used for making chemicals

Salt is important for the _chemicals industries_, which are mostly based around _Cheshire_ and _Merseyside_ because of all the _rock salt_ there. The first thing they do is _electrolyse_ it.

Rock Salt — think of the pollution as it runs into the sea...

Look at this page. There's all that writing but only about _10 important facts to learn_ in the whole lot. Hmm, I guess that's my fault — too much drivel. Still, if it makes you smile occasionally...

Electrolysis of Salt

Electrolysis of Salt gives Hydrogen, Chlorine and NaOH

Salt dissolved in water is called *BRINE*. When *concentrated brine* is *electrolysed* there are *three* useful products:

a) *Hydrogen gas* is given off at the cathode.
b) *Chlorine gas* is given off at the anode.
c) *Sodium hydroxide* is left in solution.

These are collected, and then used in all sorts of *industries* to make various products as detailed below.

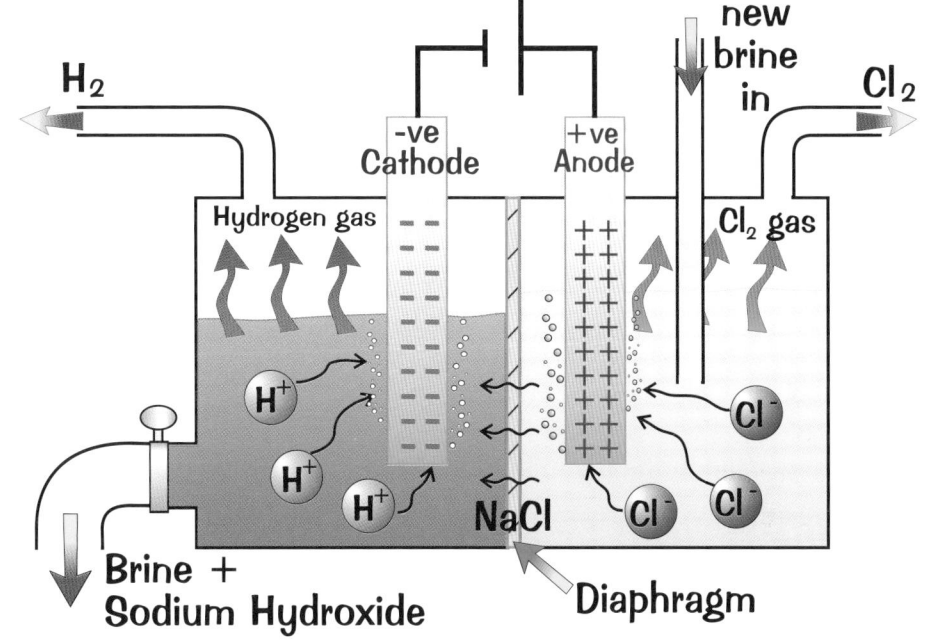

Useful Products from the Electrolysis of Brine

With all that effort and expense going into the electrolysis of brine, there'd better be some pretty useful stuff coming out of it — and so there is... and you have to learn it all too. Ace.

1) Chlorine

1) Used in *disinfectants* 2) *killing bacteria* (e.g. in *swimming pools*)
3) *plastics* 4) *HCl* 5) *insecticides*. Don't forget the simple lab test for chlorine — it *bleaches* damp *litmus paper*.

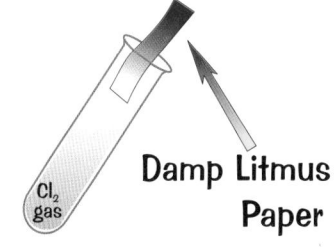

Damp Litmus Paper

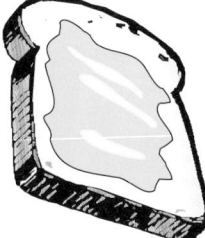

2) Hydrogen

1) Used in the *Haber Process* to make *ammonia* (remember?).
2) Used to change *oils* into *fats* for making *margarine* ("hydrogenated vegetable oil"). Think about that when you spread it on your toast in the morning. Yum.

3) Sodium hydroxide

Sodium Hydroxide is a very strong *alkali* and is used *widely* in the *chemical industry*.
e.g. 1) *soap*   2) *ceramics*   3) *organic chemicals*
      4) *paper pulp*   5) *oven cleaner*.

Learn the many uses of salt — just use your brine...

There's even *less* to learn on this page than on the last one, so you've got no excuse for not *learning it all*. Write down the products from the electrolysis of brine and suggest a few uses for each one. Believe me, you won't get much easier marks in the Exam than these. Giveaway.

Uses of Halogens

Compounds of Alkali Metals & Halogens

Some Uses of Halogens you Really Should Know

Aren't halogens and their compounds ace. _Learn and enjoy._

Fluorine, (or rather fluoride) reduces dental decay

1) _Fluorides_ can be added to drinking water and toothpastes to help prevent _tooth decay_.
2) In its natural state fluorine appears as a _pale yellow gas_.

Chlorine is used in bleach and for sterilising water

1) _Chlorine_ dissolved in _sodium hydroxide_ solution is called _bleach_.
2) _Chlorine compounds_ are also used to _kill germs_ in swimming pools and drinking water.
3) It's used to make _insecticides_ and in the manufacture of _HCl_.
4) It's also used in the manufacture of the plastic PVC (polyvinyl _chloride_)

Iodine is used as an antiseptic...

...but it stings like nobody's business and stains the skin brown. Nice.

Silver halides are used on black and white photographic film

1) _Silver_ is very _unreactive_. It does form halides but they're very _easily_ split up.
2) In fact, ordinary visible _light_ has enough energy to do so.
3) _Photographic film_ is coated with _colourless silver bromide_.
4) When light hits parts of it, the silver bromide _splits up_ into _silver_ and _bromine_:

$$2AgBr \rightarrow Br_2 + 2Ag \text{ (silver metal)}$$

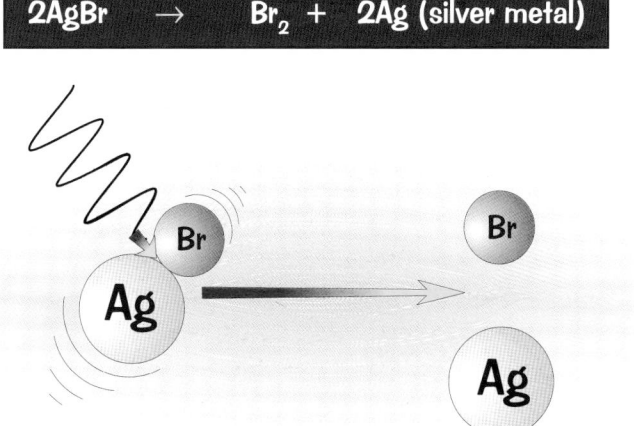

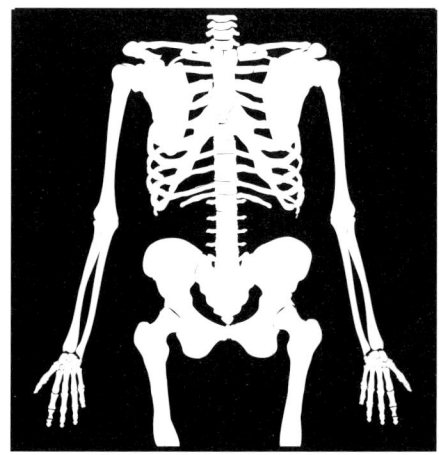

5) The _silver metal_ appears _black_. The brighter the light, the _darker_ it goes.
6) This produces a black and white _negative_, like an X-ray picture for example.

Well that's pretty much the bare bones of it anyway...

Lots of seriously tedious facts to learn here. And virtually no nonsense. But think about it, the only bit you're gonna really remember forever is that bit about iodine. _Am I right or am I right?_

Revision Summary for Section Five

*Phew, I tell you what you know — there's some serious Chemistry in Section Five.
I suppose it makes up for Section Four being so easy. This is where all the really grisly stuff is.
All I can say is, just keep trying to learn it. These jolly questions will give you some idea of how
well you're doing. For any you can't do, you'll find the answers somewhere in Section Five.*

1) What two properties did they base the early periodic table on?
2) Who was the old rogue who had the best shot at it and why was his table so clever?
3) What feature of atoms determines the order of the modern Periodic Table?
4) What are the Periods and Groups? Explain their significance in terms of electrons.
5) Draw diagrams to show the electron arrangements for the first twenty elements.
6) Explain the trend in reactivity of metals and non-metals using the notion of "shielding".
7) What are the electron arrangements of the noble gases? What are the properties of them?
8) Give two uses each for helium, neon and argon.
9) What would *you* fill an airship with: hydrogen or helium? What was Mr Zeppelin's big mistake?
10) Which Group are the alkali metals? What is their outer shell like?
11) List four physical properties, and two chemical properties of the alkali metals.
12) Give details of the reactions of the alkali metals with water and chlorine, and burning in air.
13) What colour of flame is produced when each of the alkali metals are burned in air?
14) What can you say about the pH of alkali metal oxides and hydroxides?
15) Describe the trends in appearance and reactivity of the halogens as you go down the Group.
16) List four properties common to all the halogens.
17) Give a use for each of the four halogens: fluorine, chlorine, bromine and iodine.
18) Give details, with equations, of the reaction of the halogens with metals, including silver.
19) Give details, with equations, of the displacement reactions of the halogens.
20) What is hydrogen chloride? Exactly how do you produce an acid from it?
21) Is hydrogen chloride covalent or ionic in its *natural* state? What about in acidic form?
22) List four properties of transition metals, and two properties of their compounds.
23) Name six transition metals, and give uses for three of them.
24) Describe fully the colour of universal indicator for every pH value from 1 to 14.
25) What type of ions are always present in a) acids and b) alkalis? What is neutralisation?
26) What is the equation for reacting acid with metal? Which metal(s) don't react with acid?
27) To what extent do Cu, Al, Mg, Fe and Zn react with dilute acid? What would you see?
28) When a burning splint is held over the test tubes, how loud would the different squeaky pops be?
29) What type of salts do hydrochloric acid and sulphuric acid produce?
30) Write balanced symbol equations for the reactions of HCl and H_2SO_4 with Mg, Al and Zn.
31) What type of reaction is "acid + metal oxide", or "acid + metal hydroxide"?
32) What proportion of the elements are metals? What do all metals contain?
33) Write down the twelve common metals in the order of the Reactivity Series.
34) Where do carbon and hydrogen fit in and what is the significance of their positions?
35) Describe the reaction of all twelve metals when heated in air. (Yes, *twelve*)
36) Describe the reaction of all twelve metals with water (or steam).
37) Describe the reaction of all twelve metals with dilute acid.
38) What type of reaction is this? Give two other examples, with equations.
39) List six properties of metals. List four properties of non-metals.
40) What about the oxides of non-metals — are they acidic or alkaline?
41) Draw a *detailed* diagram showing *clearly* how brine is electrolysed.
42) What are the two sources of salt and what are the three main uses of it?
43) Give uses for the three products from the electrolysis of brine.

Rates of Reaction

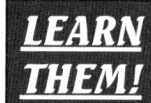
The Rate of a Reaction Depends on Four Things:

1) _TEMPERATURE_
2) _CONCENTRATION_   — (or _PRESSURE_ for gases)
3) _CATALYST_
4) _SIZE OF PARTICLES_   — (or _SURFACE AREA_)

LEARN THEM!

Typical Graphs for Rate of Reaction

The plot below shows how the speed of a particular reaction varies under _different conditions_. The quickest reaction is shown by the line that becomes _flat_ in the _least_ time. The line that flattens out first must have the _steepest slope_ compared to all the others, making it possible to spot the slowest and fastest reactions.

1) _Graph 1_ represents the original _fairly slow_ reaction. The graph is not too steep.
2) _Graphs 2 and 3_ represent the reaction taking place _quicker_ but with the _same initial amounts_. The slope of the graphs gets steeper
3) The _increased rate_ could be due to _any_ of these:

   a) increase in _temperature_
   b) increase in _concentration_ (or pressure)
   c) _catalyst_ added
   d) solid reactant crushed up into _smaller bits_.

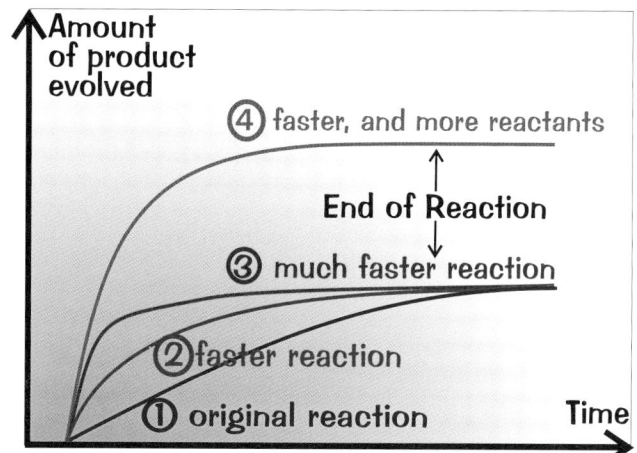

Amount of product evolved

④ faster, and more reactants

End of Reaction

③ much faster reaction

② faster reaction

① original reaction

Time

4) _Graph 4_ produces _more product_ as well as going _faster_. This can _only_ happen if _more reactant(s)_ are added at the start. _Graphs 1, 2, and 3_ all converge at the same level, showing that they all produce the same amount of product, although they take _different_ times to get there.

Reactions can go at all sorts of different rates

1) One of the _slowest_ is the _rusting_ of iron (it's not slow enough though — what about my little MGB).
2) A _moderate speed_ reaction is a _metal_ (like magnesium) reacting with _acid_ to produce a gentle stream of _bubbles_.
3) A _really fast_ reaction is an _explosion_, where it's all over in a _fraction_ of a second.

Revision of reaction rates — goes down like a bomb...

Lets face it, chemistry doesn't come much _easier_ than this. Or as _exciting_ — there's explosions, bubbles and all sorts on this page. Wow. Anyway, only a few points to learn here. Make sure you _learn_ the points in the box — and then _learn_ the rest of the page as well.

Rates of Reaction

Three ways to Measure the Speed of a Reaction

The *speed of reaction* can be observed *either* by how quickly the reactants are used up or how quickly the products are forming. It's usually a lot easier to measure *products forming*. There are *three* different ways that the speed of a reaction can be *measured*:

1) Precipitation

1) This is when the product of the reaction is a *precipitate* which *clouds* the solution.
2) Observe a *marker* through the solution and measure how long it takes for it to *disappear*.
3) The *quicker* the marker disappears, the *quicker* the reaction.
4) This only works for reactions where the initial solution is rather *see-through*.

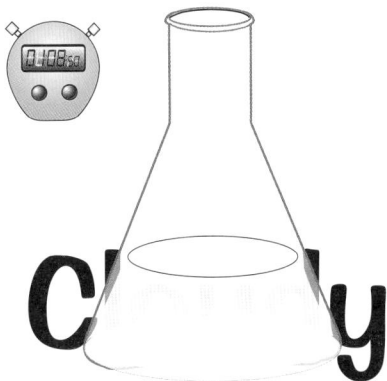

2) Change in mass (usually gas given off)

1) Measuring the speed of a reaction that *produces a gas* can be carried out on a *mass balance*.
2) As the gas is released the mass *disappearing* is easily measured on the balance.
3) The *quicker* the reading on the balance *decreases*, the *faster* the reaction.
4) *Rate of reaction graphs* are particulary easy to plot from the results from this method.
5) This is the *most accurate* of the three methods described on this page because the mass balance is very accurate.

3) The volume of gas given off

1) This involves the use of a *gas syringe* to measure the *volume* of gas given off.
2) The *more* gas given off during a given *time interval*, the *faster* the rate of reaction.
3) A graph of *gas volume* against *time elapsed* could be plotted to give a rate of reaction graph (see P.78 and P.79).

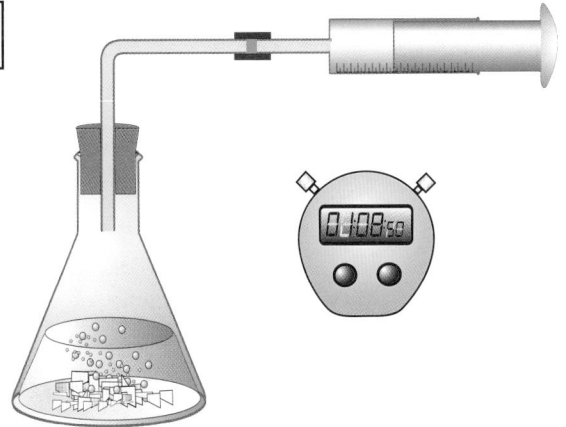

How to get a fast, furious reaction — crack a wee joke...

There's all sorts of bits and bobs of information on this page. To learn it all, you've got to learn to split it up into separate sections and do them one at a time. Practise by *covering the page* and seeing how much you can *scribble down* for each section. *Then try again, and again...*

Collision Theory

Particles need to collide to react

Reaction rates are explained perfectly by _Collision Theory_.
It's really simple. It just says:

1) The _rate_ of a reaction simply depends on how _often_ and how _hard_ the reacting particles _collide_ with each other.
2) The basic idea is that particles have to _collide_ in order to _react_.
3) They also have to collide _hard enough_.

More Collisions increases the Rate of Reaction

All _four_ methods of increasing the _rate of reactions_ as listed on P.74 can be _explained_ in terms of increasing the _number of collisions_ between the reacting particles:

1) TEMPERATURE increases the Number of Collisions

1) When the _temperature_ is _increased_ the particles all move _quicker_.
2) If they're moving quicker, they're going to have _more collisions_.
3) Even _small_ increases in temperature can have surprisingly _large_ effects on the reaction rate.
4) Since the particles are hitting each other with _greater force_, they are also more likely to react to form new products.
5) An experiment about the effect of _temperature_ on _rate of reaction_ is detailed overleaf.

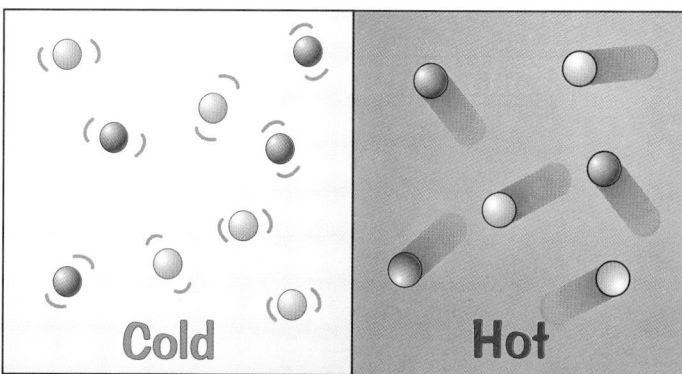

2) More CONCENTRATION (or PRESSURE) Means more Collisions

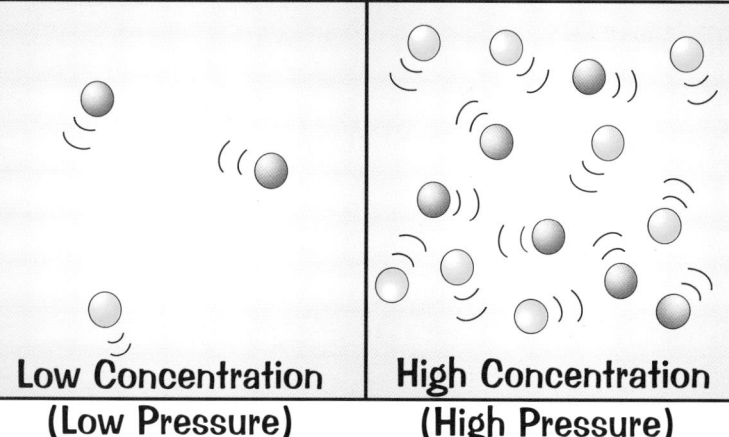

1) If the solution is made more _concentrated_ it means there are more particles of _reactant_ knocking about between the water molecules.
2) This makes collisions between the _important_ particles _more likely_.
3) If the particles are _more likely_ to collide, then they are _more likely_ to react.
4) Hence an _increase_ in concentration causes an _increase_ in reaction rate.

5) In a _gas_, increasing the _pressure_ means the molecules are _more squashed up_ together so there are going to be _more collisions_.

Collision Theory

3) Increasing the SURFACE AREA increases the Collisions

1) If one of the reactants is a _solid_ then
   breaking it up into _smaller_ pieces will
   increase its surface area.
2) This means the particles around it in the
   solution will have _more_ area to work on
   so there'll be _more_ useful collisions.
3) Remember, more collisions means
   quicker reactions.

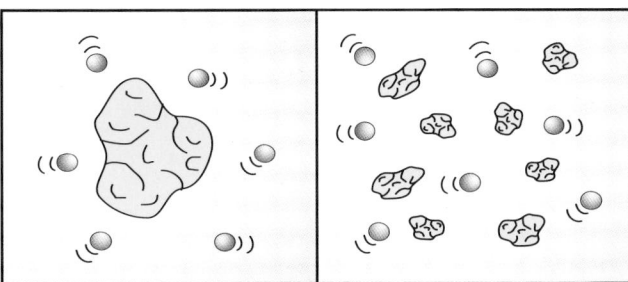

4) A CATALYST increases the Number of Collisions

1) A _catalyst_ works by giving the _reacting_
   particles a _surface_ to _stick to_ where
   they can _bump_ into each other.
2) This obviously increases the _number of_
   collisions too.
3) For more on catalysts and how they
   affect reaction rates, see P.80.

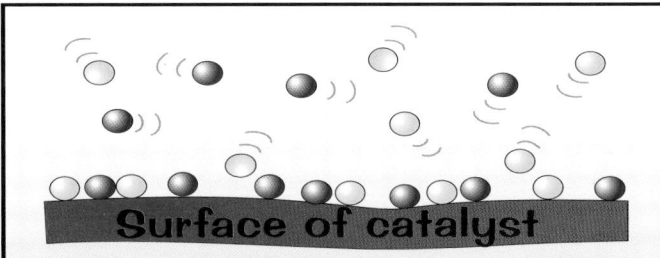

Surface of catalyst

Faster Collisions increase the Rate of Reaction

Higher temperature also increases the _energy_ of the collisions, because it makes all the particles
move _faster_. It is _only_ higher temperature (and _not_ surface area, concentration or the presence
of a catalyst) that _increases_ the particle's energy — remember that for the Exam.

Faster collisions are ONLY caused by increasing the temperature

1) Reactions _only_ happen if the particles collide with
   enough energy.
2) At a _higher temperature_ there will be _more_
   particles colliding with _enough energy_ to make the
   reaction happen.
3) This _initial_ energy is known as the _activation_
   energy, and it's needed to _break_ the initial bonds.
   (See P. 88)
4) Once the activation energy has been reached, the
   reaction has _enough energy_ to _start_.

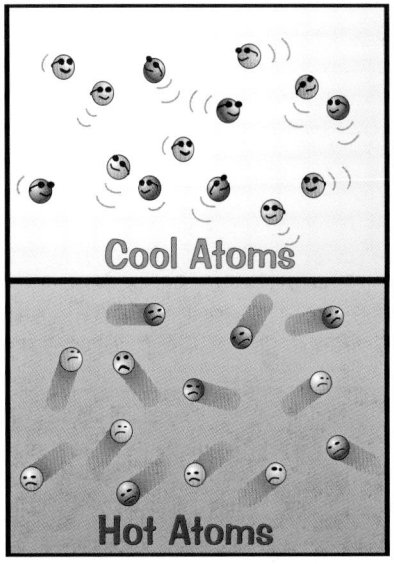

Cool Atoms

Hot Atoms

Collision Theory — I reckon it's always women drivers...

This is quite easy I think. Isn't it all kind of obvious — at least once you've been told it, anyway.
The more often particles collide and the harder they hit, the greater the reaction rate. There's a
few extra picky details of course (isn't there always!), _but you've only got to LEARN them..._

Rate of Reaction Experiments

REMEMBER: *Any reaction* can be used to investigate *any* of the four factors that affect the *rate*.
These pages illustrate *four important reactions*, but only *one factor* has been considered for each.
But we could just as easily use, say, the marble chips/acid reaction to test the effect of *temperature* instead.

1) Reaction of Hydrochloric Acid and Marble Chips

This experiment is often used to demonstrate the effect of *breaking* the solid up into *small bits*.

1) Measure the *volume* of gas evolved with a *gas syringe* and take readings at *regular intervals*.
2) Make a *table of readings* and plot them as a *graph*.
3) *Repeat* the experiment with *exactly the same* volume of *acid*, and *exactly the same* mass of *marble* chips, but with the marble *more crunched up*.
4) Then *repeat* with the same mass of *powdered chalk* instead of marble chips.

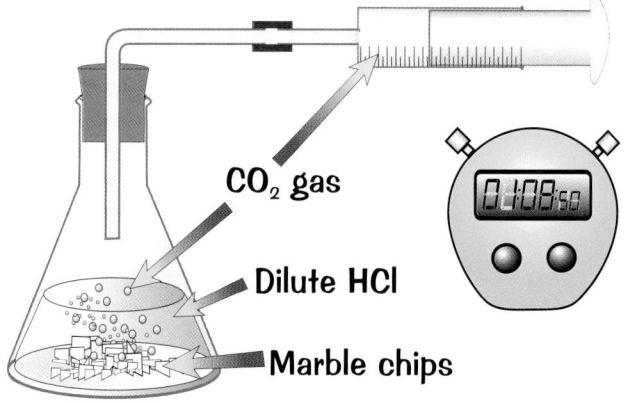

CO_2 gas

Dilute HCl

Marble chips

This graph shows the effect of using finer particles of solid

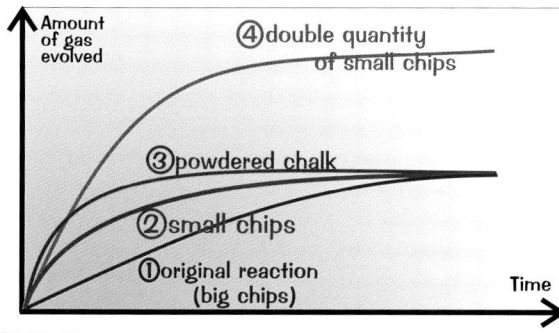

Amount of gas evolved
④ double quantity of small chips
③ powdered chalk
② small chips
① original reaction (big chips)
Time

1) The increase in *surface area* causes *more collisions* so the rate of reaction is *faster*.
2) *Line 4* shows the reaction if a *greater mass* of small marble chips is added.
3) The *extra surface area* gives a *quicker reaction* and there is also *more gas evolved* overall.

2) Reaction of Magnesium Metal With Dilute HCl

1) *This reaction* is good for measuring the effects of *increased concentration* (as is the marble/acid reaction).
2) This reaction gives off *hydrogen gas*, which we can measure with a *mass balance*, as shown.
   (The other method is to use a gas syringe, as above.)

This graph shows the effect of using stronger acid solutions

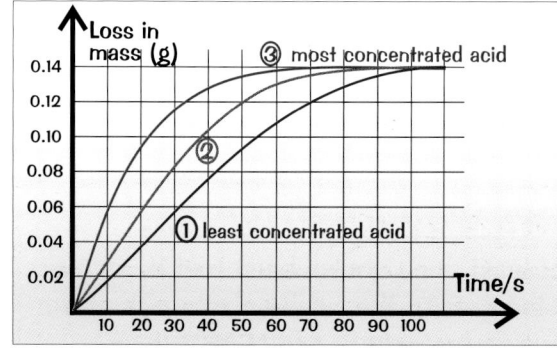

Loss in mass (g)
③ most concentrated acid
②
① least concentrated acid
Time/s
0.02 0.04 0.06 0.08 0.10 0.12 0.14
10 20 30 40 50 60 70 80 90 100

1) Take *readings* of mass at *regular* time intervals.
2) Put the results in a *table* and work out the *loss in mass* for each reading. *Plot a graph*.
3) *Repeat* with *stronger* acid solutions but always with the *same* amount of magnesium.
4) The *volume* of acid must always be kept *the same* too — only the *concentration* is increased.
5) The three graphs show the *same* old pattern. *Higher* concentration giving a *steeper graph* with the reaction *finishing* much quicker.

Rate of Reaction Experiments

3) Sodium Thiosulphate and HCl produce a Cloudy Precipitate

1) These two chemicals are both _clear solutions_.
2) They react together to form a _yellow precipitate_ of _sulphur_.
3) The experiment involves watching a black mark _disappear_ through the _cloudy sulphur_ and _timing_ how long it takes to go.

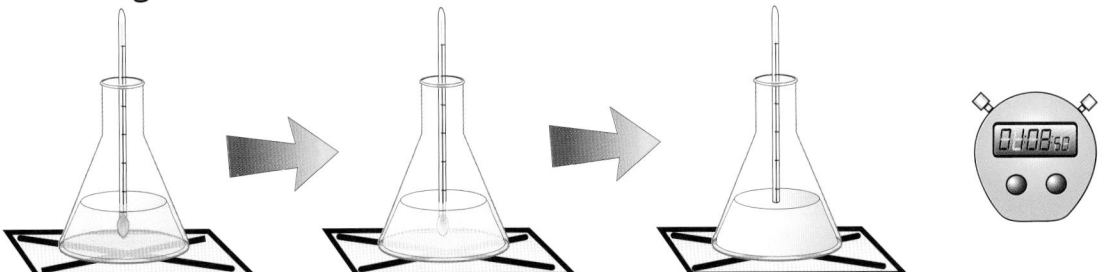

4) The reaction can be _repeated_ for solutions at different _temperatures_.
5) The _depth_ of liquid must be kept the _same_ each time, of course.
6) The results will of course show that the _higher_ the temperature the _quicker_ the reaction and therefore the _less time_ it takes for the mark to _disappear_. These are typical results:

Temperature	20°C	25°C	30°C	35°C	40°C
Time taken for mark to disappear	193s	151s	112s	87s	52s

This reaction can _also_ be used to test the effects of _concentration_.
One sad thing about this reaction is it _doesn't_ give a set of graphs. Well I think it's sad. All you get is a set of _readings_ of how long it took till the mark disappeared for each temperature. Boring.

4) The Decomposition of Hydrogen Peroxide

This is a _good_ reaction for showing the effect of different _catalysts_.
The decomposition of hydrogen peroxide is:

$$2H_2O_2 \rightleftharpoons 2H_2O + O_2$$

1) This is normally quite _slow_ but a sprinkle of _manganese(IV) oxide catalyst_ speeds it up no end. Other catalysts which work are a) _potato peel_ and b) _blood_.
2) _Oxygen gas_ is given off which provides an _ideal way_ to measure the rate of reaction using the good ol' _gas syringe_ method.

O₂ gas
Hydrogen peroxide
Catalyst

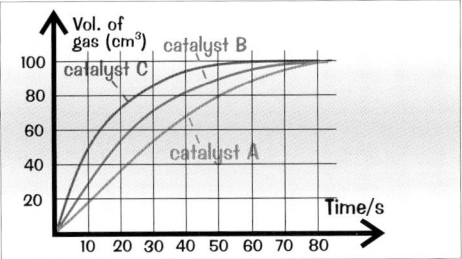

1) Same old graphs of course.
2) _Better_ catalysts give a _quicker reaction_ which is shown by a _steeper graph_ which levels off quickly.
3) This reaction can also be used to measure the effects of _temperature_, or of _concentration_ of the H_2O_2 solution. The graphs will look just the same.

Four Top Rate Reactions — learn and enjoy...

There's always so much happening with reaction rates. Is it products or reactants we're looking at? Are we measuring gas, or mass, or cloudiness? Is it the effect of temp. or conc. or catalyst or surface area we're investigating? There's just so much going on, _but you'll just have to sort it all out and learn it_.

Catalysts

Many reactions can be _speeded up_ by adding a _catalyst_.

A _CATALYST_ is a substance which _INCREASES_ the speed of a reaction, without being _CHANGED_ or _USED UP_ in the reaction.

Higher

1) Catalysts lower the Activation Energy

1) Catalysts _lower_ the _activation energy_ (see P. 88) of reactions, making it _easier_ for them to happen.
2) This means a _lower temperature_ can be used.

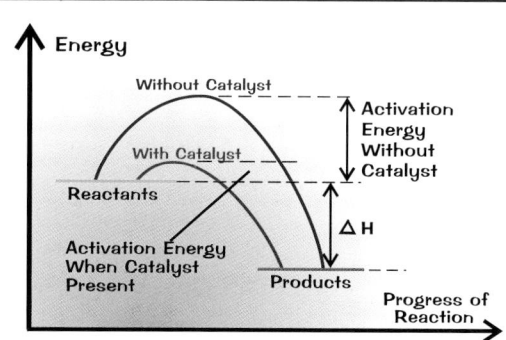

2) Catalysts work best when they have a Big Surface Area

1) Catalysts are usually used as a _powder_ or _pellets_ or a _fine gauze_.
2) This gives them _maximum surface area_ to enable the reacting particles to _meet up_ and do the business.

Catalyst Powder   Catalyst Pellets   Catalyst Gauzes

3) Catalysts Help Reduce Costs in Industrial Reactions

1) _Catalysts_ increase the rate of many _industrial reactions_, which saves a lot of _money_ simply because the plant doesn't need to operate for _as long_ to produce the _same amount_ of stuff.
2) Alternatively, a catalyst will allow the reaction to work at a _much lower temperature_ and that can save a lot of money too. Catalysts are therefore _very important_ for _commercial reasons_.
3) Catalysts are used _over and over_ again. They may need _cleaning_ but they don't get _used up_.
4) Different _reactions_ use different _catalysts_.
5) _Transition metals_ are common catalysts in many _industrial_ reactions. _Know these two_:

a) An Iron Catalyst is used in the Haber Process

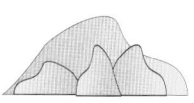

$$N_{2(g)} + 3H_{2(g)} \xrightarrow{\text{Iron Catalyst}} \rightleftharpoons 2NH_{3(g)}$$

(See P. 26 and P. 85–86)

b) A Platinum Catalyst is used in the production of Nitric Acid

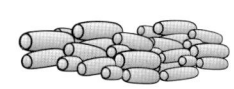

Ammonia + Oxygen $\xrightarrow{\text{Platinum Catalyst}}$ Nitrogen monoxide + Water

(See P. 27)

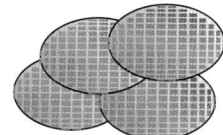

Catalysts are like great jokes — you can use them over and over...

Make sure you _learn the definition_ in the top box _word for word_. The fact is they can easily ask you: "What is a catalyst?" (2 Marks). This is much easier to answer if you have a "word for word" definition at the ready. If you don't, you're likely to lose half the marks on it. That's a fact.

Biological Catalysts

Enzymes are Biological Catalysts

1) _Living things_ have thousands of different chemical processes going on inside them.
2) The _quicker_ these happen the _better_, and raising the _temperature_ of the body is an important way to _speed them up_.
3) However, there's a _limit_ to how far you can _raise_ the temperature before _cells_ start getting _damaged_, so living things also produce _enzymes_ which act as _catalysts_ to _speed up_ all these chemical reactions without the need for _high temperatures_.

Enzymes are produced by Living Things and are Great

1) Every _different_ biological process has its _own enzyme_ designed especially for it.
2) Enzymes have _two main advantages_ over traditional _non-organic_ catalysts:
   a) They're _not scarce_ like many metal catalysts e.g. platinum.
   b) They _work best_ at low temperatures, which keeps costs down.

EXAMPLES: _"biological"_ washing powders and _dishwasher_ powders.

Enzymes _Like it_ Warm but _Not Too Hot_

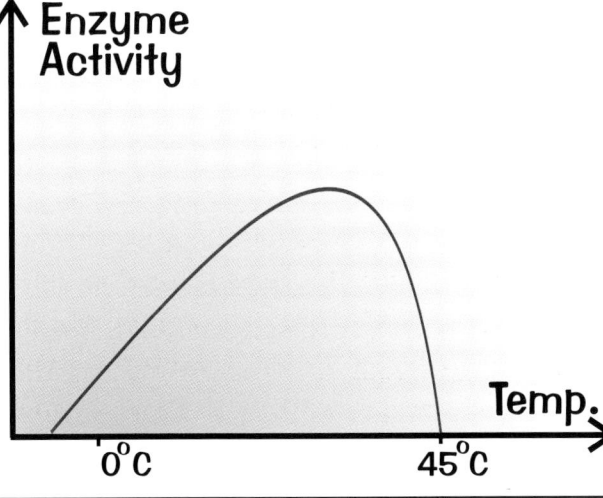

1) The _chemical reactions_ in _living cells_ are _quite fast_ in conditions that are _warm_ rather than _hot_.
2) This is because the cells use _enzyme_ catalysts, which are _protein molecules_.
3) Enzymes are usually _damaged_ by temperatures above about _45°C_, and as the graph shows, their activity drops off _sharply_ when the temperature gets _a little too high_.

Freezing food stops the Enzyme Activity (and the Bacteria)

1) At _lower_ temperatures, enzyme activity also _drops_ quite quickly.
2) This is the idea behind _refrigeration_, where foods are kept at about _4°C_ to keep _enzyme_ and _bacterial_ activity _to a minimum_ so that food stays _fresher_ for _longer_.
3) _Freezers_ store food at about _-20°C_ and at this temperature bacteria and enzymes _don't function_ at all.
4) However, they're not destroyed by _freezing_ and once the food _thaws out_ they spring back into action. So frozen food should be _thawed carefully_ and then _cooked again_ before eating.
5) Cooking _destroys_ all bacteria and enzymes, so _properly cooked_ food is _safe to eat_.
6) However, even _cooked_ foods will go off _pretty rapidly_ if left in a _warm_ place.

"Enzymes" — sounds like a brand of throat lozenge...

This page is definitely a candidate for the mini-essay method. Two mini-essays in fact. What else is there to say? _Scribble down the facts, then look back and see what you missed._

82

Uses of Enzymes

Reactions Involving Enzymes

Living cells use chemical reactions to produce _new materials_. Many of these reactions provide products which are _useful_ to us. Here are _three_ important examples:

Yeast in Brewing of Beer and Wine: Fermentation

1) _Yeast cells_ convert _sugar_ into _carbon dioxide_ and _alcohol_.
2) They do this using the enzyme _ZYMASE_.
3) The main thing is to keep the _temperature_ just right.
4) If it's _too cold_ the enzyme won't work very _quickly_.
5) If it's _too hot_ it will _destroy_ the enzyme.
6) This biological process is called _fermentation_ and is used for making alcoholic drinks like _beer and wine_.

FERMENTATION is the process of _yeast_ converting _sugar_ into _carbon dioxide_ and _alcohol_.

$$\text{Glucose} \xrightarrow{\text{Zymase}} \text{Carbon dioxide} + \text{Ethanol} \quad (+ \text{Energy})$$

Yeast in Bread-making: Fermentation again

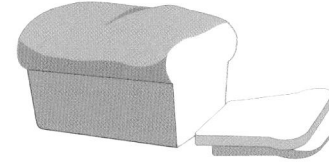

1) The reaction in _bread-making_ is _exactly the same_ as that in _brewing_.
2) Yeast cells use the enzyme _zymase_ to break down sugar and this gives them _energy_.
3) It also releases carbon dioxide gas and alcohol as waste products.
4) The _carbon dioxide gas_ is produced _throughout_ the bread mixture and forms in _bubbles_ everywhere.
5) This makes the bread _rise_ and gives it its familiar texture. The small amount of alcohol also gives the bread some extra flavour, no doubt.
6) When the bread is put in the oven the yeast is _killed_ and the _reaction stops_.

Yoghurt making — only pasteurised milk

1) _Pasteurised milk_ **MUST** be used for making _yoghurt_, because _fresh_ milk contains many _unwanted bacteria_ which would give them a _bad taste_.
2) Instead the pasteurised milk is mixed with _specially grown cultures_ of bacteria.
3) This mixture is kept at the _ideal temperature_ for the bacteria and their enzymes to work.
4) For _yoghurt_ this is _pretty warm_ at about _45°C_.
5) The _yoghurt-making bacteria_ convert _lactose_, (the natural sugar found in milk), into _lactic acid_. This gives yoghurts their slightly _bitter_ taste.

With a face like that you could be Chief Curdler in a yoghurt factory, you could pal.

This page is just so easy— it's a blummin' picnic...

This is rapidly turning into a Domestic Science book. Anyway, you're expected to know all these details of making bread, wine, cheese and yoghurt. _Mini-essays again, I'd say._ Enjoy.

Simple Reversible Reactions

A _reversible reaction_ is one which can go _in both directions_.
In other words the _products_ of the reaction can be _turned back_ into the original _reactants_.
Here are some _examples_ you should know about in case they spring one on you in the Exam.

The Thermal decomposition of Ammonium Chloride

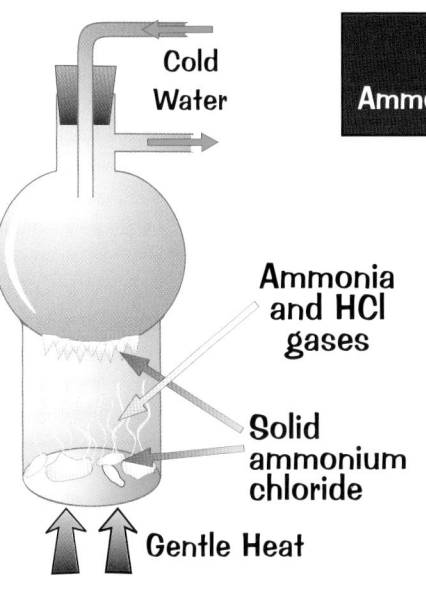
Cold
Water

Ammonia
and HCl
gases

Solid
ammonium
chloride

Gentle Heat

$$NH_4Cl_{(s)} \rightleftharpoons NH_{3(g)} + HCl_{(g)}$$
Ammonium chloride $\rightleftharpoons$ ammonia + hydrogen chloride

1) When _ammonium chloride_ is _heated_ it splits up into _ammonia gas_ and _HCl gas_.

2) When these gases _cool_ they recombine to form _solid ammonium chloride_.

3) This is a _typical reversible reaction_ because the products _recombine_ to form the original substance _very easily_.

The Thermal decomposition of hydrated copper sulphate

1) Good old dependable _blue copper(II) sulphate_ crystals here again.
2) Here they're displaying their usual trick, but under the guise of a _reversible reaction_.

3) If you _heat them_ it drives the water off and leaves _white anhydrous_ copper(II) sulphate powder.

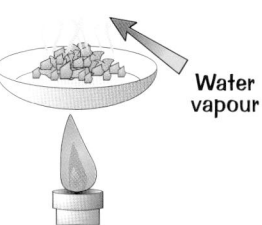
Water
vapour

4) If you then _add_ a couple of drops of _water_ to the _white powder_ you get the _blue crystals_ back again.

The proper name for the _blue crystals_ is _Hydrated Copper(II) sulphate_.   _"Hydrated"_ means _"with water"_.   When you drive the water off they become a white powder, _Anhydrous copper(II) sulphate_.   _"Anhydrous"_ means _"without water"_.

Reacting Iodine with Chlorine to get Iodine Trichloride

There's quite a jolly _reversible reaction_ between the mucky brown liquid of _iodine monochloride_ (ICl), and nasty green _chlorine gas_ to form nice clean yellow crystals of _iodine trichloride_ (ICl_3).

$$ICl + Cl_2 \rightleftharpoons ICl_3$$

  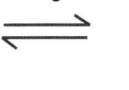 

1) Which way the reaction goes depends on the _concentration_ of chlorine gas in the air around.
2) A _lot_ of chlorine will favour formation of the _yellow crystals_.
3) A _lack_ of chlorine will encourage the crystals to _decompose_ back to the horrid brown liquid.

Learn these simple reactions, then see what you know...

These reactions might seem a bit obscure but they're all mentioned in one syllabus or another, so any of them could come up in your Exam. There really isn't much to learn here. _Scribble it._

Reversible Reactions in Equilibrium

A _reversible reaction_ is one where the _products_ can react with each other and _convert back_ to the original chemicals. In other words, _it can go both ways_.

> **A _REVERSIBLE REACTION_ IS ONE WHERE THE _PRODUCTS_ OF THE REACTION CAN _THEMSELVES REACT_ TO PRODUCE THE _ORIGINAL REACTANTS_**
>
> A + B ⇌ C + D

Reversible Reactions will reach Dynamic Equilibrium

1) If a reversible reaction takes place in a _closed system_ then a state of _equilibrium_ will always be reached.

2) _Equilibrium_ means that the _relative (%) quantities_ of reactants and products will reach a certain _balance_ and stay there. A '_closed system_' just means that none of the reactants or products can _escape_.

3) It is in fact a _DYNAMIC EQUILIBRIUM_, which means that the reactions are still taking place in _both directions_ but the _overall effect is nil_

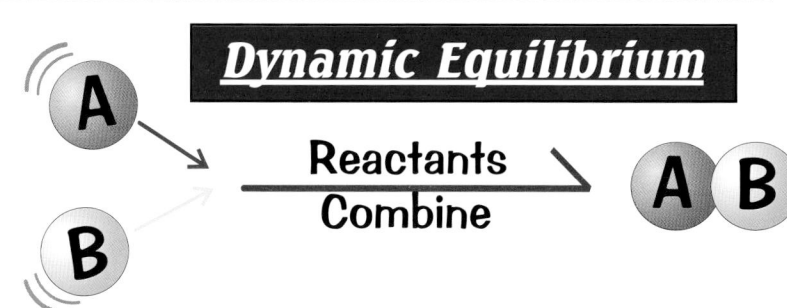

Dynamic Equilibrium

Reactants Combine

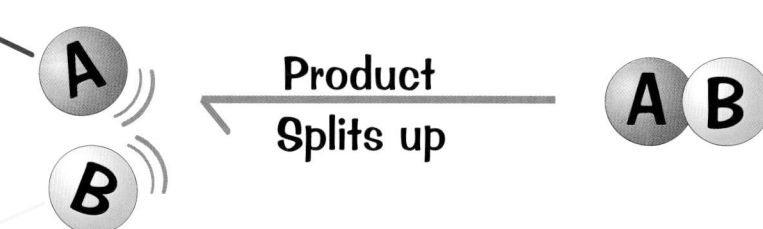

Product Splits up

because the forward and reverse reactions _cancel_ each other out.
The reactions are taking place at _exactly the same rate_ in both directions.

Changing Temperature and Pressure to get More Product

1) In a reversible reaction the '_position of equilibrium_' (the relative amounts of reactants and products) depends _very strongly_ on the _temperature_ and _pressure_ surrounding the reaction.

2) If we _deliberately alter_ the temperature and pressure we can _move_ the "position of equilibrium" to give _more product_ and _less_ reactants.

Two Very Simple Rules for which way the equilibrium will move

1) All reactions are _exothermic_ in one direction and _endothermic_ in the other.
If we _raise_ the _temperature_, the _endothermic_ reaction will increase to _use up_ the extra heat.
If we _reduce_ the _temperature_ the _exothermic_ reaction will increase to _give out_ more heat.

2) Many reactions have a _greater volume_ on one side, either of _products_ or _reactants_.
If we _raise_ the _pressure_ it will encourage the reaction which produces _less volume_.
If we _lower_ the _pressure_ it will encourage the reaction which produces _more volume_.

Learning/forgetting— the worst reversible of them all...

There's three sections here: the definition of a reversible reaction, the notion of dynamic equilibrium and two equilibrium rules. Make sure you can give a good rendition of all of them.

The Haber Process Again

Remember way back on P.26 when you first stumbled across the Haber Process? Bet you thought that was the last you'd see of it. _Wrong_. Trouble is, the reaction between hydrogen and nitrogen in the Haber Process is _reversible_, which means you've got to look at it again in this section too. Lovely.

The Haber Process is a controlled Reversible Reaction

The Equation is:

$$3H_{2\,(g)} + N_{2\,(g)} \rightleftharpoons 2NH_{3\,(g)}$$

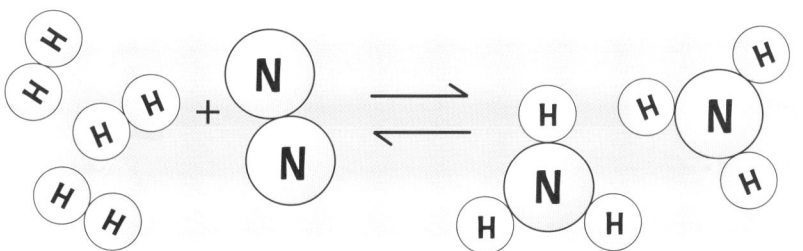

The _forward_ reaction here is _exothermic_

Higher Pressure will Favour the Forward Reaction so build it strong...

1) On the _left side_ of the equation there are _four moles_ of gas (N_2 + $3H_2$), whilst on the _right side_ there are just _two moles_ (of NH_3).

2) So any _increase_ in _pressure_ will favour the _forward reaction_ to produce more _ammonia_. Hence the decision on pressure is _simple_. It's just set _as high as possible_ to give the _best % yield_ without making the plant _too expensive_ to build. 200 to 350 atmospheres are typical pressures used.

Lower Temperature WOULD favour the forward Reaction BUT...

The reaction is _exothermic_ in the forward direction which means that _increasing_ the temperature will actually move the equilibrium _the wrong way_, away from ammonia and more towards H_2 and N_2. But they _increase_ the temperature anyway... this is the tricky bit so learn it real good:

LEARN THIS REAL WELL:

1) The _proportion_ of ammonia at equilibrium can only be increased by _lowering_ the temperature.
2) But instead they _raise_ the temperature and accept a _reduced_ proportion (or _yield_) of ammonia.
3) The reason is that the _higher_ temperature gives a much higher _RATE OF REACTION_.
4) It's better to wait _20 seconds_ for a _10% yield_ than to have to wait _60 seconds_ for a _20% yield_.
5) Remember, the unused hydrogen, H_2, and nitrogen, N_2, are _recycled_ so _nothing is wasted_.

Learning the Haber process — it's all ebb and flow...

If they're going to use any reversible reaction for an Exam question, the chances are it's going to be this one. The trickiest bit is that the temperature is raised not for a better equilibrium, but for increased speed. Try the mini-essay method to _scribble down all you know_ about equilibrium and the Haber process.

The Haber Process Again

Last page on the Haber Process. Hang in there!

The Iron Catalyst *Speeds up the reaction and keeps costs down*

1) The *iron catalyst* makes the reaction go *quicker* which gets it to the *equilibrium proportions* more quickly. But don't forget that the catalyst *doesn't* affect the *position* of equilibrium (i.e. the % yield). *Remember* that iron is one of the *transition metals* and that the transition metals are commonly used as catalysts.

2) *Without the catalyst* the temperature would have to be *raised even further* to get a *quick enough* reaction and that would *reduce the % yield* even further. So the catalyst is very important.

Maximising *the product is a matter of* compromise

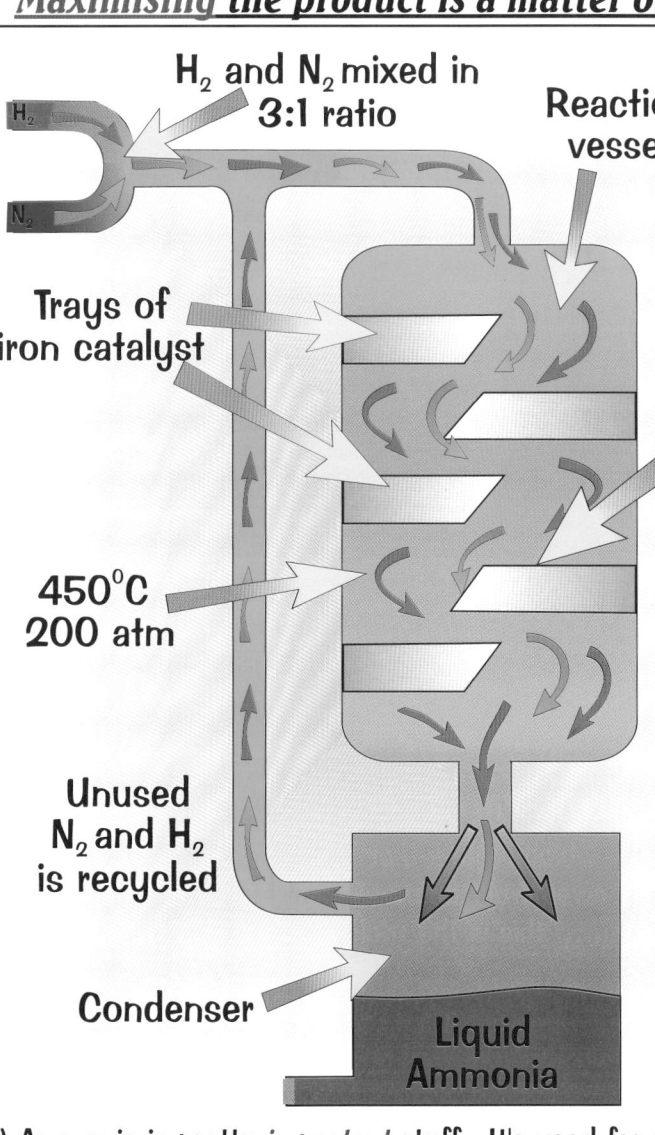

H₂ and N₂ mixed in 3:1 ratio

Reaction vessel

Trays of iron catalyst

This is where the Reversible Reaction takes place

450°C 200 atm

Unused N₂ and H₂ is recycled

Condenser

Liquid Ammonia

1) *Removing product* would be an effective way to improve yield because the reaction keeps *chasing equilibrium* while the product keeps *disappearing*. Eventually *the whole lot* is converted.

2) This *can't be done* in the Haber Process because the ammonia can't be removed until *afterwards* when the mixture is *cooled* to *condense out* the ammonia.

3) The reaction is *exothermic*, and the heat given out is used to heat up *fresh supplies* of nitrogen and hydrogen (*before* they enter the reacting vessel) to *speed up* their rate of reaction.

4) Ammonia is pretty *important* stuff. It's used for making ammonium nitrate *fertiliser*, which is a big part of modern farming. That's why the Haber Process is so important, and why *you* have to learn so much about it.

Learn it — then you can Haber rest...

That's the last on the mighty Haber Process I'm afraid. I know how much you'll miss it after your Exams have finished. Only a *few simple points* to learn here — make sure you remember how the *catalyst* affects the reaction, and how to *maximise* the yield of ammonia. Yes, you know the routine by now — *get scribbling and learn it all*.

Energy Transfer in Reactions

Whenever chemical reactions occur *energy* is usually *transferred* to or from the *surroundings*.

In an *Exothermic* Reaction, Heat is GIVEN OUT

> An *EXOTHERMIC REACTION* is one which *GIVES OUT ENERGY* to the surroundings, usually in the form of *HEAT* and usually shown by a *RISE IN TEMPERATURE*

1) *Burning Fuels*

The best example of an *exothermic* reaction is *burning fuels*.
This obviously gives out a lot of heat — it's very exothermic.

2) *Neutralisation reactions*

Neutralisation reactions (acid + alkali) are also exothermic.

3) *Crystal formation*

Addition of water to anhydrous *copper(II) sulphate* to turn it
into blue crystals *produces heat*, so it must be *exothermic*.

ACID

Steam

Don't do
it like this!!

ALKALI

In an *Endothermic* Reaction, Heat is TAKEN IN

> An *ENDOTHERMIC REACTION* is one which *TAKES IN ENERGY* from the surroundings, usually in the form of *HEAT* and usually shown by a *FALL IN TEMPERATURE*

Endothermic reactions are *less common* and less easy to spot.
So *LEARN* these three examples, in case they ask for one:

1) *Photosynthesis* is endothermic

— it *takes in energy* from the sun.

Energy

2) *Dissolving certain salts* **in water**

e.g. 1) potassium chloride   2) ammonium nitrate

Salt
cubes

Food

3) *Thermal decomposition*

Heat must be supplied to cause the compound to *decompose*. The best
example is converting *calcium carbonate* into *quicklime* (see P. 28).

$$CaCO_3 \rightarrow CaO + CO_2$$

A lot of heat energy is needed to make this happen. In fact the
calcium carbonate has to be *heated in a kiln* and kept at
about *800°C*. It takes almost *30,000kJ* of heat to make
10kg of calcium carbonate decompose.
That's pretty endothermic I'd say, wouldn't you.

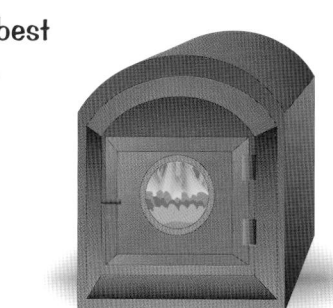

Take a leaf out of my book — get learning...

An easy page to get you started on energy transfers. It's pretty much common sense really
— some reactions like to *give energy out* (usually in the form of heat) and some like to *take energy in*.
Just because you're used to reactions that give *out* heat doesn't mean they're all like that. Anyway,
enough of this waffle. Know what you need to do now? Yip, you guessed it, *get learning*. *NOW*.

Energy Transfer in Reactions

ΔH LOOKS A BIT ODD, sure, but it's really not that bad. It just represents the *"heat of reaction"*.

If ΔH *IS NEGATIVE* (-ve), it means *heat is given out* (exothermic).

If ΔH *IS POSITIVE* (+ve), it means *heat is taken in* (endothermic).

It's as simple as that.

Energy Level Diagrams show if it's Exo- or Endo-thermic

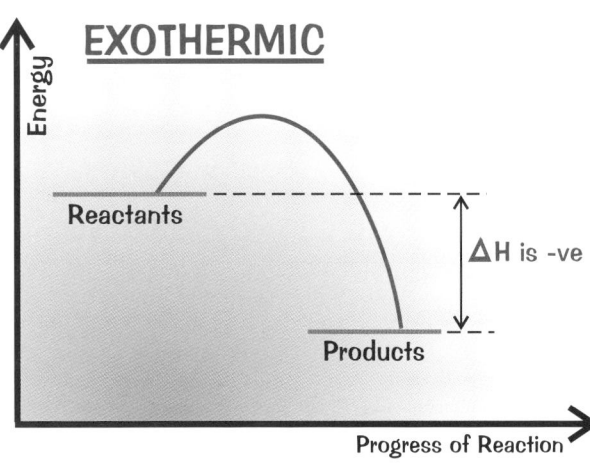

In Exothermic Reactions ΔH is -ve

1) This diagram shows an *exothermic reaction* because the products are at a *lower energy* than the reactants.
2) The difference in *height* represents the energy *given out* in the reaction (per mole). A reaction that gives energy out is exothermic. ΔH is -ve in this case.
3) The *initial rise* in the line represents the energy needed to *break* the old bonds. This is the *activation energy*.

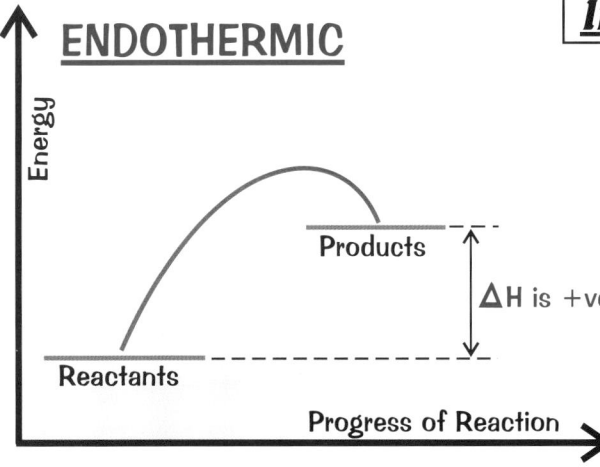

In Endothermic Reactions ΔH is +ve

1) This diagram shows an *endothermic reaction* because the products are at a *higher energy* than the reactants.   ΔH is +ve.
2) The *difference in height* represents the *energy taken in* during the reaction.
3) The graph shows that the products end up at a *higher energy* than the reactants, meaning that energy has been *taken in* — an *endothermic* reaction.

The Activation Energy is Lowered by Catalysts

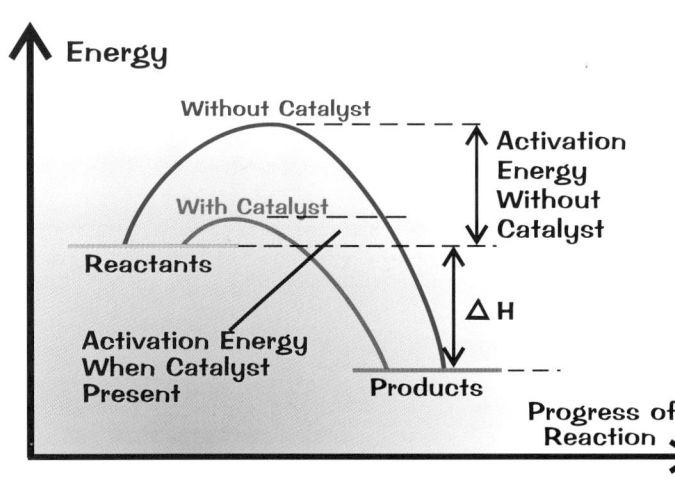

1) The *activation energy* represents the *minimum energy* needed by reacting particles for the reaction to occur.
2) A *catalyst* makes reactions happen *easier* (and therefore quicker) by *reducing* the initial energy needed.
3) This is represented by the *lower curve* on the diagram showing a *lower activation energy*.
4) The *overall energy change* for the reaction, ΔH, *remains the same* though.

Energy Transfer in Reactions

Energy Must Always be _Supplied_ to _Break bonds..._
...and Energy is Always Released When Bonds Form

1) During a chemical reaction, _old bonds_ are _broken_ and _new bonds_ are _formed_.

2) Energy must be _supplied_ to break _existing bonds_ — so bond breaking is an _endothermic_ process.

3) Energy is _released_ when new bonds are _formed_ — so bond formation is an _exothermic_ process.

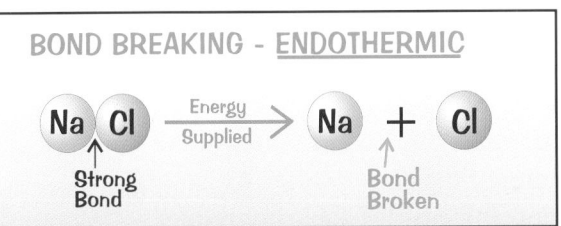

BOND BREAKING - ENDOTHERMIC

Na Cl → Na + Cl

Strong Bond | Energy Supplied | Bond Broken

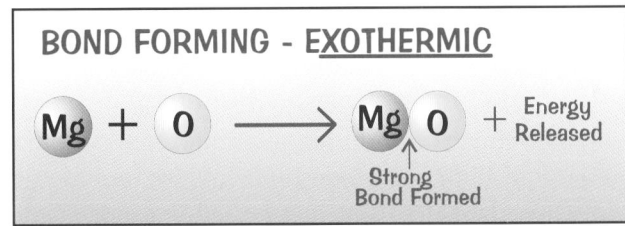

BOND FORMING - EXOTHERMIC

Mg + O → Mg O + Energy Released

Strong Bond Formed

4) In an _exothermic_ reaction, the energy _released_ in bond formation is _greater_ than the energy used in _breaking_ old bonds.

5) In an _endothermic_ reaction, the energy _required_ to break old bonds is _greater_ than the energy _released_ when _new bonds_ are formed.

Bond Energy Calculations — need to be _practised!_

1) _Every_ chemical bond has a particular _bond energy_ associated with it.

2) This _bond energy_ is always the same no matter what compound the bond occurs in.

3) We can use these _known bond energies_ to calculate the _overall energy change_ for a reaction.

4) You need to _practise_ a few of these, but the basic idea is really very simple.
   Practise the example below until you can do it completely on your own:

Example: _The Formation of HCl_

The bond energies you need are:
H—H +436kJ/mole;
Cl—Cl +242kJ/mole;
H—Cl 431kJ/mole.

$$H_2 + Cl_2 \rightarrow 2HCl$$

Using these known bond energies you can _calculate_ the _energy change_ for this reaction:

1) _Breaking_ one mole of H—H and one mole of Cl—Cl bonds _requires_ 436 + 242 = _+678kJ_

2) _Forming two_ moles of H—Cl bonds _releases_ 2×431 = _862kJ_

3) _Overall_ there is more energy _released_ than used: 862 – 678 = _184kJ/mol_ released.

4) Since this is energy _released_, then if we wanted to show ΔH we'd need to put a _–ve_ in front of it to indicate that it's an _exothermic_ reaction, like this: | ΔH = _-184kJ/mol_ |

Energy transfers and Heat — make sure you take it in...

The stuff about exothermic and endothermic reactions is really quite simple. You've just got to get used to the big words. The bond energy calculations though, now they need quite a bit of practice, as do any kind of calculation questions. You can't just do one or two and think that'll be OK. No way man, you've gotta do loads of them. I'm sure "Teach" will provide you with plenty of practice though. Good old "Teach"!

Higher Higher Higher

Higher Higher Higher

Revision Summary for Section Six

This section isn't too bad really. I suppose some of the stuff on Rates of Reaction and Equilibrium gets a bit chewy in places, but the rest is all a bit of a breeze really, isn't it? Anyway, here's some more of those nice easy questions which you enjoy so much. Remember, if you can't answer one, look at the appropriate page and learn it. Then go back and try them again. Your hope is that one day you'll be able to glide effortlessly through all of them — it's a nice trick if you can do it.

1) What are the four factors which the rate of reaction depends on?
2) What are the three different ways of measuring the speed of a reaction?
3) Explain how each of the four factors that increase the rate of a reaction increase the *number of collisions* between particles.
4) What is the other aspect of collision theory which determines the rate of reaction?
5) Which is the only physical factor which affects this other aspect of the collisions?
6) What happens when hydrochloric acid is added to marble chips?
7) Give details of the two possible methods for measuring the rate of this reaction.
8) Sketch a typical set of graphs for either of these methods.
9) Describe in detail how you would test the effect on the reaction rate of
       a) finer particles of solid   b) stronger concentration of acid   c) temperature
10) What happens when sodium thiosulphate is added to HCl? How is the rate measured?
11) Write down the equation for the decomposition of hydrogen peroxide.
12) What is the best way to increase the rate of this reaction?
13) What is the best way to measure the rate of this reaction? What will the graphs look like?
14) What is the definition of a catalyst? What does a catalyst do to the activation energy?
15) Name two specific industrial catalysts and give the process they are used in.
16) What are enzymes? Where are they made? Give three examples of their use by man.
17) Sketch the graph for enzyme activity vs temperature, indicating the temperatures.
18) What effect does freezing have on food? What happens when you thaw it out?
19) Give the word-equation for fermentation. Which organism and which enzyme are involved?
20) Explain what happens in brewing and bread-making. What is the difference between them?
21) What kind of milk is needed for making cheese and yoghurt and why?
22) What gives yoghurt and cheese their flavour?
23) What is a reversible reaction? Describe three simple reversible reactions involving solids.
24) Explain what is meant by dynamic equilibrium in a reversible reaction.
25) How does changing the temperature and pressure of a reaction alter the equilibrium?
26) How does this influence the choice of pressure for the Haber Process?
27) What determines the choice of operating temperature for the Haber process?
28) What effect does the catalyst have on the reaction?
29) Give three examples of exothermic and three examples of endothermic reactions.
30) Draw energy level diagrams for these two types of reaction.
31) How do bond breaking and bond forming relate to these diagrams?
32) What are bond energies and what can you calculate from them?

Answers

P.31 *1)* Fe_2O_3 (s) + $3H_2$(g) → $2Fe$(s) + $3H_2O$(l)   *2)* $6HCl$ (aq) + $2Al$(s) → $2AlCl_3$(aq) + $3H_2$(g)
P.33 *1)* Cu=64, K=39, Kr=84, Fe=56, Cl=35.5 *2)* NaOH=40, Fe_2O_3=160, C_6H_{14}=86, $Mg(NO_3)_2$=148
P.34 *1)* *a)* 30.0% *b)* 88.9% *c)* 48.0% *d)* 65.3% *2)* CH_4 *P.35* *1)* 21.4g *P.36* *1)* 3.75 litres *2)* 5.67g *P.37* 15,333cm³

P.38 Revision Summary *2) a)* $CaCO_3$(s) + 2HCl (l) → $CaCl_2$(aq) + H_2O (l) + CO_2(g) *b)* Ca (s) + $2H_2O$ (l) → $Ca(OH)_2$(aq) + H_2(g)
c) H_2SO_4 (aq) + 2KOH (aq) → K_2SO_4 (aq) + $2H_2O$ (l)   *d)* Fe_2O_3 (s) + $3H_2$ (g) → 2Fe (s) + $3H_2O$ (g)
e) C_3H_8 (g) + $5O_2$ (g) → $3CO_2$ (g) + $4H_2O$ (g)   *6) a)* 40 *b)* 108 *c)* 44 *d)* 84 *e)* 106 *f)* 81 *g)* 56 *h)* 17 *i)* 58 *j)* 58.5 *k)* 127
7) a) 40.0% *b) i)* 12.0% *ii)* 27.3% *iii)* 75.0% *c) i)* 74.2% *ii)* 70.0% *iii)* 52.9%
10) a) Fe_2O_3 *b)* CaF_2 *c)* C_5H_{12} *d)* $MgSO_4$ *11) a)* 186.8g *b)* 80.3g *c)* 20.1g *12)* The molar mass, i.e. M_r in g
13) a) 48 litres *b)* 11.2 litres *c)* 150 litres *d)* 6.3g *e)* 8.6g *14) a)* 5.25g *b)* 37.5 litres

Index

Index